Kansas City Ballet

Rachel Coats in
Toccata e due canzoni (2005)

KANSAS CITY BALLET

THE FIRST FIFTY YEARS

By Wyatt Townley

Foreword by Jacques d'Amboise

ROCKHILL
BOOKS

Kansas City, Missouri

Kansas City Ballet: The First Fifty Years copyright © 2007
by Kansas City Ballet. All rights reserved.

Edited by Donna Martin
Design by Brian Grubb

ROCKHILL
B O O K S

Published by Rockhill Books,
An imprint of The Kansas City Star Co.
1719 Grand Blvd., Kansas City, Missouri 64108

ISBN: 978-1-933466-43-9

Library of Congress Control Number: 2007930323

Printed in the United States of America by
Walsworth Publishing Co. Inc.,
Marceline, Missouri

Rachel Coats in *Voyager* (2006)
PHOTO BY KENNY JOHNSON

CONTENTS

FOREWORD

by Jacques d'Amboise

This year's a natal celebration for Kansas City Ballet.

How do you start a ballet company? You must be energetic, determined, a visionary, a teacher, a choreographer, a director, a manager, a fundraiser, an inspiration, a diplomat, and let's face it, you need two things above all: a heavy dollop of madness and a silver bucket full of luck. If you're missing anything in that formula, nothing will take root and flower. Tatiana Dokoudovska did it, but not easily. There were the ups and downs, roller-coaster curves and foothills to mount, but she succeeded and Kansas City did it with her. That's one thing you can say about that city. Its citizens have a stick-to-itiveness and an integrity that's a model for all.

Back in New York in the late fifties we all knew about the KC Ballet because of "The Duke," Tatania's brother. If any dancer wanted the most challenging of classes they went to the Ballet Arts School in Carnegie Hall where Dokoudovsky, "The Duke," reigned supreme.

"I'll stay here, Tatiana. You can have the rest of the country!" The Duke probably suggested. Who knows? In any case she went west and found Kansas City and established the Kansas City Ballet.

But who was going to take the baton from the capable hands of Tatiana and lead KC Ballet from the late twentieth century into the twenty-first? *Hurray!* They found Todd Bolender.

I first saw Todd dance in 1946 in Ballet Society and he stole the show as the Fox in *Renard*. Then he starred in Balanchine's *Symphony Concertant* and in the ballet *The Four Temperaments*. In that seminal Balanchine masterpiece, Todd established a mark that is at the top of Mount Everest. World-famous dancers have danced his roles magnificently but they never reached the summit to stand with Todd. He was a master of the theater arts and did everything you can imagine in the world of performance, ballet in particular.

In 1953 NYC Ballet was touring Italy. Todd and I shared most of the major roles in the repertoire. In Trieste, Italy, amid riots on the streets, we were doing a matinee. After the matinee I was taking a leave of absence from the company to fly to Hollywood to play one of the brothers in the movie *Seven Brides for Seven Brothers*. Todd and I had just finished dancing *Interplay*, Jerome Robbins's strenuous ballet,

(clockwise from left) Deena Budd, Susan Manchak and Louise Nadeau in *Les Sylphides* (1988)

and Todd had collapsed in the wings. He was lying on top of a giant orange wooden crate that carried the ballet company's costumes and was exhausted, wheezing with bronchitis and coughing blood. I felt so guilty leaving. "Todd, I'm so sorry. I won't be here to cover for you." Todd managed a wan smile and panted out, "It's all right, Daisy" (my nickname in NYC Ballet). "I'll make it, I'll go on. Isn't that what we do?"

It was decades later, in 1996, when Todd passed on the baton to William Whitener. A very precious and weighty charge. Take, guide, and love this ballet company. Keep it healthy, labor always to keep the environment for the dancers and the art of the ballet to flourish.

I danced for more than thirty years before I asked myself the questions, What is dance? What is its relationship to music? What is art, anyway? I came up with some thoughts to answer my own questions.

Dance is a form of communication that expresses emotion through the ordering of gesture and movement, in space and in time. Music is a form of communication that expresses emotions through the ordering of sound in time. They are the stuff of the universe.

The welling up of emotion seeking expression through the arts opens your heart and mind to possibilities that are limitless. They are pathways that touch upon our brains and emotions. They are human beings' greatest form of communication. They walk in tandem with those other two giants, science and play, and best describe what it's like to be human. Arts, science, and play are central to our culture. They invent and shape and are necessary components to evolution. Everyone should dance. Everyone should make music. Each day without music drains a drop from the soul. But only the chosen few should become dancers and musicians. For when you seek that path, you sign up for a lifetime of unyielding dedication, discipline, and pain, the crucible that transforms the person into the artist.

In dance, ballet holds a unique place. It is the one dance form that attempts to deny gravity. It is the art of the aerial; off the ground it inhabits the higher place, the magical, the mysterious, the glorified, past the Van Allen belt.

Those who place themselves in service to the art of ballet are to be treasured.

Recently I had the privilege of coming to visit Kansas City to attend a memorial for Todd. I visited with management and board members, hung out with William, toured parts of the city, and best of all, watched the dancers perform. They were superb, and William is to be lauded for his artistic direction. How thrilling it was for me to see dance, in particular ballet, which I hold so close to my heart, established and flourishing here, gracing the city and holding out its promise for future generations.

With my love and admiration to
Kansas City and its Ballet.

Yours,

Jacques d'Amboise

Jacques d'Amboise

Jacques d'Amboise works in the studio with Kansas City Ballet dancers in 1984

Louise Nadeau and Brian Staihr
in *Classical Symphony* (1987)

Chelsea Teel and
Geoffrey Kropp in
Great Galloping Gottschalk (200

This book is for Mette Spaniardi
who taught me the world of difference between a straight knee
and a bent one.

– W.T.

ACKNOWLEDGMENTS

The author would like to thank Lisa Hickok for early leadership in bringing this book into being, Donna Martin for valiant and salient editing, Doug Weaver and *The Kansas City Star* for access to archives, Karen Bowser for tactical assistance, James Jordan for his steadfastness and generosity, Michele Hamlett-Weith for entrusting sacred scrapbooks, Steve Short for long ago pointing the way, Larry Redding for his bad karma, Russell Baker for his good counsel, Grace Townley for lunches in Lawrence, all the interviewees for ransacking their brains and hearts for the stories that made this real, the understanding friends who were neglected during this project, and finally, Roderick Townley, who brought the author vats of coffee, while reminding her to look up.

Kansas City Ballet would like to thank the following for their assistance in reviewing the book's accuracy: Kevin Amey, Jeffrey J. Bentley, Karen Bowser, Carol Feiock, Michele Hamlett-Weith, Lisa Schubert Hickok, Trula Hunt, James Jordan, Jean Quick Murphy, Wendy Powell, Jennifer Wampler, and William Whitener.

We also thank those who participated in the interview process: Kevin Amey, Christopher Barksdale, Jeffrey J. Bentley, Martin Cohen, Kimberly Cowen, Flo Klenklen, Michele Hamlett-Weith, Elizabeth Hard-Simms, Lisa Schubert Hickok, James Jordan, Una Kai, Michael Kaiser, Julia Irene Kauffman, Linda Martin, Jean Quick Murphy, Matthew Powell, Wendy Powell, Vicki Allen Reid, Francisco Renno, Sarah Rowland, Tenley Taylor, Lisa Thorn, Paul Tyler, Shirley Weaver, Martha Ullman West, William Whitener, and Elizabeth Wilson.

Kansas City Ballet would like to thank the following photographers for the use of the photos reproduced in this book: Jim Barcus, Fred Blocher, Martha Dimeo/Hallmark, Dale Durfee, Gross Photo Industries, Carter Hamilton, Kathe Hamilton, Delores Johnson, Kenny Johnson, Shane Keyser, Kevin Manning, Don Middleton, Beau Pierce, Jim Sczepanski, David Smalls, Strauss-Peyton Inc., Mary Watkins Photography, Wilborn & Fitzgeralds, and Steve Wilson. Every effort has been made to locate photographers, and any additional credits will be included in future printings.

PHOTO BY KENNY JOHNSON

Chelsea Teel in *Pas de Dix* (2007)

John Charles Smith
and Dolly Allard in
Symphonic Metamorphosis (1975)

ONE

THE
DOKOUDOVSKA
ERA

At its essence, dance is the art of vanishing. Each bend of the knee disappears into the leap that follows it. One step dissolves into the inevitable next, the performance moving from the limbs of the dancer to the eyes of the audience, who disperse in the night. Too soon the artists themselves move on, their brief candles having burned so brightly.

Steps change; casts change; names change; but after fifty years of determination and dauntless dreaming, the Kansas City Ballet is alive and kicking. May this book serve as a tribute to the spirit and dedication of all who forged the way here: the hands that sewed the tutus, the feet that bled, the choreographers who pulled movement out of air, the supporters whose generosity paved the way from the invisible to the visible and back. There are thousands such people, making the art available to millions over the past five decades.

May it remind all who saw even a single program that what happened here matters – that grace, however fleeting, is possible. The art may be forever disappearing, but its footprints are everywhere in these pages. In particular, this book celebrates the perseverance of three quite different pioneers – Tatiana Dokoudovska, Todd Bolender, and William Whitener – who have cumulatively led the Kansas City Ballet to where it now stands: a nationally acclaimed professional company with twenty-five dancers, a diverse repertory, and (soon) a permanent home near the historic Union Station.

With more than six hundred students in the Kansas City Ballet School on two campuses, the troupe is investing in its future through the promise of its dancers-in-training. Having struggled through the pains of birth and five decades of growth, Kansas City Ballet has earned its place as a nexus of the Midwest's cultural life, at the still point of the turning world. In T.S. Eliot's words,

Except for the point, the still point,
There would be no dance, and there is only the dance.

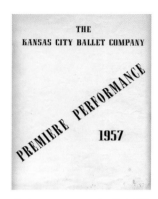

Debut program, April 1957

WHAT'S IN A NAME?

In its end is its beginning. Incorporated as Kansas City Ballet in 1957, the company has come full circle to return to the name it started with fifty years ago. Before its incorporation, it was called Kansas City Civic Ballet to emphasize its semiprofessional nature, then dropped the "Civic" on becoming a professional troupe. In 1986, it was retitled State Ballet of Missouri to reflect an expanding regional presence, with St. Louis functioning as a second home. Then in 2000, it reclaimed its original name, which for the purposes of this book, we'll use throughout.

A CIRCUITOUS ARRIVAL

Kansas City Ballet (KCB) began with the arrival of a small woman with raven hair and a riveting gaze. In town from New York for a stint at Starlight Theatre, Tatiana Dokoudovska was no typical corps member, but a complex artist with a history to match. Born in 1921 in Beausoleil, France, to a Russian nobleman and an Italian aristocrat, she migrated to Paris and New York, and through a labyrinth of heartbreaking circumstances found her way to Kansas City.

Dokoudovska's artistic lineage had prepared her well for the work ahead. Her grandfather, an operatic tenor, had sung with world-renowned soprano Adelina Patti. Her mother was a godchild and student of acclaimed Russian ballerina Olga Preobrajenska, and her father an actor and director.

Stranded in France by the Russian Revolution, her exiled father set to work as a taxi driver while her mother toured Europe as a ballroom dancer. The family doctor prescribed physical exercise for Tatiana and her brother, Vladimir, who were sent off to Preobrajenska's ballet class in Paris. By age twelve, Tatiana was performing, and at fifteen, touring Europe with her mother, brother, and cousin in Ballet Russe de l'Opera Comique.

"Hitler was starting up at the time," she said in an interview with *The Kansas City Star*. "We saw him while traveling in Germany. We were terrified because our company directors were Jewish."

Politics, war, and illness would play large roles in the decisions that ultimately led the young dancer here. After appearing with various companies including the Ballet Russe de Monte Carlo, Tatiana accepted an invitation from Lucia Chase to join what is now American Ballet Theatre. In 1939, at age seventeen, she crossed the ocean on a refugee passport.

The company rented a house on Fifty-fourth Street in New York, and Miss Chase assembled a constellation of dance luminaries to choreograph on the group, including Michel Fokine, Bronislava Nijinska, Antony Tudor, Anton Dolin, Agnes de Mille, and Eugene Loring. Tatiana danced with the company for two years, usually partnered by Jerome Robbins.

But war again intervened. With no funds and a diminishing roster of just eight dancers, Ballet Theatre disbanded for the duration of World War II. Tatiana took a job with the ballet company at Radio City Music Hall, staying an intermittent seven years. She returned to Europe to dance with Ballet Russe at Covent Garden, surviving in bombed-out London on "small portions of meat and one egg a month," she recalled in a *Star* interview. "Still, it was a fantastic season. People were starving, but they came to the ballet and stood in long lines at the stage door for autographs."

When Tatiana returned to the States, she became an American citizen. Her career had zigzagged around the world, and was punctuated by illness. Childhood bouts of tonsilitis and rheumatic fever were followed by a burst appendix, dislocated toes, and pneumonia, all of which took a psychological toll. Before accepting Lucia Chase's invitation to return to Ballet Theatre as a soloist, she took a summer stock job with Starlight Theatre in Kansas City to build her confidence.

Once here, she never left.

Tatiana Dokoudovska (1957)

STAYING TO CHANGE

Were it not for Wiktor Labunski, Tatiana Dokoudovska might well have returned to Ballet Theatre, and the Kansas City Ballet would never have materialized. Unlikely events coalesced. During Starlight's 1954 season, she did a television interview; Dr. Labunski (then director of what is now the University of Missouri – Kansas City Conservatory of Music and Dance) saw that interview and offered her a teaching contract at the Conservatory. She said yes.

"I found here a world I thought had been destroyed during World War II," she recalled. "I thought I was in heaven – the grass, the trees, the beauty and refinement. One Sunday I walked to the Nelson Art Gallery and threw a coin into the wishing well in Rozzelle Court. I wished that I could stay in Kansas City. It must have been destiny, because suddenly things began to happen."

Dokoudovska would become the head of the Conservatory's dance division, and a stern disciplinarian. Hair was to be subdued into a bun. Skirts and ruffles were banned for streamlined leotards and tights. Once class started, the doors shut and no latecomers were admitted. Also not allowed: talking, bathroom breaks, or leaving fifth position between exercises. The sounds in the studio got louder, with squalls of Russian-accented commands and the sudden thunder of a stick striking the floor.

"In the '50s and '60s there was no money for a pianist to play for classes," explained Vicki Allen Reid, longtime dancer with the company who would become its ballet mistress, rehearsal director, and resident den mother. "So Miss Tania used the stick: 'One! Two!' That's what we trained to – a stick beating on the floor!"

The timid scattered, and enrollment plummeted from three hundred to seventy-five in the first year. Undaunted and determined to raise the bar at the Conservatory, "Miss Tania" (as she was known to her pupils) eschewed traditional dance recitals for full-length ballets. No surprise that this taskmaster was a direct descendent of Russian czar Ivan the Terrible. One dancer put Miss Tania's legendary tactics to use in the delivery room, conjuring up memories of rehearsals to help her withstand the painful labor of her first child. "Rehearsals were much worse," she recalled.

PHOTO BY KATHE HAMILTON

Miss Tania teaching class in Treadway Hall

But underlying the intensity of Dokoudovska's teaching style was a love of the art and a passion to kindle it in others. "Dance has been like oxygen to my life," she said in an interview. "I breathe it. It exhilarates me."

Eventually, the message behind the fireworks got out. Over the span of three years, enrollment climbed back to 230, and 25 of the most promising became the fledgling first version of the Kansas City Ballet.

DEBUT OF A DREAM

The company had its premiere performance on April 30, 1957, at the Victoria Theater (now the Lyric). On the program were two full-length ballets: Michel Fokine's original *Les Sylphides* (Tania having been in his first cast) and *Ruse d'Amour*, a Dokoudovska adaptation of Fokine's *The Toys*. *Ruse* was a humorous look at romance in which a girl feigns rejection of her lover, who in turn pretends to jump into a well. Other offerings included *Trio of Modern Dances Set to Medieval Themes* by Howard Vogel, Leonide

3

4

(upper left) Russ Vogler (1977-78)

(above) Carol Kindell and William Carlyle as
Estrella and Florestan in *Carnaval* (1962)

(left) Connie Salley and Edward Mann in
Michel Fokine's *Les Sylphides* (1957)

Massine's original "Tarantella" from *La Boutique Fantasque*, and the Silver Fairy variation from *The Sleeping Beauty*.

From any angle, the debut was a success. The lead from the *Kansas City Times* review: "Freshness and verve of young dancers set the pace at the premiere performance of the Kansas City Ballet company last night at the Victoria Theater. This venture, envisioning the company as a permanent, high-caliber troupe of professional proportions, won the warm approval of an audience of 1,100."

The foundation was laid. Incorporated in December 1957 as a 501(c)(3) not-for-profit organization, the troupe boasted a board of directors, business manager, and musical director. While Dokoudovska reigned as artistic director, no job was too big – or too small. She choreographed and rehearsed until 11 p.m. each night, then went home to cut patterns and sew costumes – even hand-painting the intricate lace around cuffs and hems. As for money, she funded productions out of her own pocket.

"I don't buy lavish clothes," she once said. "I invest in the Civic Ballet."

No detail was overlooked. "Miss Tania would make sure we did our makeup just like at Ballet Russe," remembers Reid, who had danced on Broadway, toured with Tony Bennett, and appeared with opera ballet companies. "We used to have to bead our eyelashes. We had to melt the black wax over a little flame, and then you'd take your hairpin and get just that little dot on there, and one at a time, you would apply that little waxy dot on the end of each eyelash. Who knew? But that's what they did for centuries in Europe and Russia."

The early years were based around two annual productions, a December *Nutcracker* and a spring season. In time, the troupe also began to tour regionally and present educational programs. The idea was twofold: go into schools to reach children who would in turn create audiences.

Meanwhile, the Conservatory dance division had built its enrollment to seven hundred, and in 1962, became the sixteenth collegiate school in the country to establish a bachelor of arts degree program in dance. A ballet or modern dance emphasis was offered, with a four-year curriculum of 125 credit hours including dance technique and theory, composition, dance history, partnering, character dance, costuming, stage makeup, lighting, supervised studio teaching, music, drama, and French.

Miss Tania
checking makeup

Shirley Weaver and Robert Sullivan in *Aurora's Wedding*

In 1967, Dokoudovska brought in Shirley Weaver, whom she'd met in New York dancing at Radio City Music Hall Ballet. Weaver was a seasoned performer, having danced for many years with Ballet Russe de Monte Carlo, Metropolitan Opera Ballet, and the Slavenska-Franklin Company.

"First it was, 'Why don't you come to class?'" Weaver said of the progressive series of invitations Miss Tania issued. "Then, 'Why don't you substitute for me today?' Then, 'Why don't you dance with the company?'" Miss Shirley, as she was known to students, became indispensable – performing with KCB, becoming an occasional choreographer and honorary ballet mistress, and pairing with Tania to fortify the ballet program at the Conservatory. Its burgeoning dance department was linked to the success of the company because it became in effect the troupe's feeder school.

GROWING PAINS

With each triumph came new challenges. "Every year we made an accomplishment," said Dokoudovska, "but every year I'd wait with my heart pounding in my toes." Not surprisingly, the main issue was money. The cost of orchestras in particular was the greatest challenge, along with the need for better dancers – and more male dancers.

"There are never enough boys," groaned her brother, Vladimir Dokoudovsky, who sometimes performed and assisted his sister with choreography and staging. "It is very difficult to continually find subjects suitable for eighteen girls and only six boys."

The company made much out of little. Among the lessons Miss Tania stressed: Doing the utmost with limited means not only built character, but paradoxically improved production quality as well. "We didn't have fancy sets to set the scene," said Jean Quick Murphy, a veteran company member who danced Dokoudovska's original role in *Les Sylphides*. "So if you wanted to bring about an aura or a sense of place, you had to be able to do it through the dancing. You really had to *be* the sylph to make it happen."

Since Dokoudovska had worked directly with Michel Fokine when he created *Les Sylphides*, she could convey his intent to her dancers. "I really understood the Romantic style from her," said Elizabeth Hard-Simms of her ten-year tenure with the company, "because she was such a fabulous coach....She really knew what Fokine wanted."

The work was its own reward. "It didn't make any difference how hard the work was, or how much we got yelled at or how many blisters we had to deal with – it was a tremendous atmosphere to be in," recalled Michele Hamlett-Weith, longtime KCB dancer throughout the seventies, who decades later would care for Tatiana at the end of her life. "We were allowed to flourish depending on how hard we were going to work."

A community was growing around the young company. For every dancer devoted to its cause, friends and family who wanted to be part of a bigger undertaking helped with costumes and sets. Mothers banded together to form the Women's Guild (now the Kansas City Ballet Guild), whose twofold purpose was fund-raising and awareness-raising. A citywide poster contest for *Nutcracker* was held in elementary schools, culminating in a public art show. Winners received savings bonds and the glory of seeing their names in the paper. Even the mayor got on board, proclaiming a special "Civic Ballet Week" in 1970.

The Guild strove to create imaginative fund-raisers, and black-tie events offered unusual twists. One gala, "La Bal Bayou," featured a gourmet dinner and costume party New Orleans style, with hanging greenery, fountains, and singing birds. Castanets and maracas set the tone for "El Mexico Magico" paired with a silent art auction from local artists and galleries. Not all fund-raisers were social events: Diehards sold nuts for *Nutcracker* at performances and shopping centers.

New costumes designed by Vince Scosolotti for *The Nutcracker* (1976)

6

Edward Villella, Patricia McBride, Tatiana Dokoudovska, Shirley Weaver, and Vladimir Dokoudovsky

Company photo 1975. Top row: Dawn Parrish, Anita Porte, Patricia Frizzell, Jean Q. Niedt, Lisa Merrill, Richard Orton. Standing: Peggy Ply, Dolly Allard, Linda Lyon, Mary Lynn Soli, Debrah Shore, Stephen Eads, Michele Hamlett, Lois Scanlon, Lisa Swanson, John Wells, Benecia Carmack, Flora Hall, William Stannard, Laura Ply, Toinette Biggins. Seated: Sandie Balot, Deborah Ummel, Carl Welander, Melissa Kelly, Nita Watson, John Smith, Kelli Buckles. Not present for picture: Wendy Macafee, Francis Wardle, Curtis Sykes, Maryhelen Hanson, Shelly Holmes.

PHOTO BY CARTER HAMILTON

Over the first two decades, many stellar guest artists and choreographers were brought in to work with the young company, growing the audience and nurturing the dancers. Among those gracing the stage in this era were Vladimir Dokoudovsky, Nathalie Krassovska, Patricia McBride, Edward Villella, Melissa Hayden, Jacques d'Amboise, Gelsey Kirkland, Merrill Ashley, Christine Redpath, Jean-Pierre Bonnefoux, David Howard, Fernando Bujones, Naomi Sorkin, Veronica Tennant, Violette Verdy, Peter Martins, Kay Mazzo, Helgi Tomasson, Starr Danias, Sallie Wilson, Valery Panov, and Galina Panova.

Ballet history was being made in Kansas City as the regional ballet movement was dawning. In 1972, the troupe hosted the first-ever Festival of the Mid-States Regional Ballet Association, with companies from eleven states gathering to take classes, audition, and share their work at the Music Hall in concert and gala performances. Five years

later, Patricia McBride of New York City Ballet would dance her first *Giselle* with KCB.

In the mid seventies, Dokoudovska fostered an across-the-board reorganization to create a fully professional company. A fall program was added, augmenting *Nutcracker* and spring offerings, creating a three-production season. For the first time, subscription season tickets were sold, and the Kansas City Philharmonic Orchestra played live for performances.

(left) Dokoudovska rehearsing the Spanish Dance from *The Nutcracker* (Michele Hamlett, center)

Dokoudovska in the Carriage House teaching preballet

7

Children in *The Nutcracker* (December 1974)

After decades at KCB's helm, Dokoudovska was ready to release her managerial duties and return to a deeper love: teaching. She would remain at the Conservatory for thirty-five years, retiring in 1989 as professor emerita, and reigning as grand dame of the regional dance scene until her death in 2005. Her many students filled the ranks of not just Kansas City Ballet, but New York City Ballet, American Ballet Theatre, Joffrey Ballet, Harkness, National Ballet in Washington, D.C., San Francisco Ballet, BalletMet, Urban Bush Women, Garth Fagan Dance Company, and the Alvin Ailey American Dance Theatre, among many others.

Tatiana Dokoudovska had borne the city a ballet company. Now someone was needed to take the troupe to the next level. It took a while to find the right person – two directors came and went in the span of four years – and change was partnered by challenge. Vicki Allen Reid's role had morphed from performer to ballet mistress in her nearly two-decade history with the group. By the end of her tenure, she was wearing multiple hats – giving company classes while keeping morale up and the repertoire in shape. "Vicki was the anchor," said Flo Klenklen, a veteran dancer who would administrate the future KCB school.

Administratively, the company was making great strides. One sign of its entry into the elite ranks of professional American dance companies was its acceptance into the Dance Touring Program of the National Endowment for the Arts. Another milestone: Dancers were paid a weekly salary "with benefits," including medical coverage and shoes.

The growing pains weren't over. But Kansas City Ballet had pecked through its eggshell and found its way to its feet. Flight was inevitable. ■

Ann Fouts, Sarah Hall, Karen Lorhan, and Elizabeth Hard in *Pas de Quatre*

Flora Hall, Russ Vogler, and
Carol Harrison in *Reflections* (1977)

Ruse d'Amour, adapted by Dokoudovska from
Fokine's *The Toys* for the premiere performance
of the Kansas City Ballet on April 30, 1957

Mayor Ilus Davis proclaims
"Civic Ballet Week."
From left, Mayor Davis,
Tom Steinhoff,
Tatiana Dokoudovska,
and Shirley Weaver

Michele Hamlett (1976)

Kansas City Ballet dancers perform
John Clifford's *Balletto* (1976)

Jean Quick Niedt, Sherrie Quinton,
Melissa Kelly, Richard Noble, and
Maryhelen Hanson in James DeBolt's
The House of the Rising Sun, 1979

Mystic Journey, choreographed
by Ronald M. Sequoio (1980)

Vicki Allen Reid's
Traversal Tapestry
performed in 1975

Eric Hyrst's *Tangents* performed in 1977

Cecilia Rodarte and Mervin Crook, Connie Salley and Edward Mann, and Mitzie Pace and John Desiderio in the Czardas from *Swan Lake*, performed with the Kansas City, Kansas, Symphony Orchestra conducted by Leopold Shopmaker (1957)

Dennis Landsman's *Aftermath* performed in 1975

Susan Lewis and William Dunne in
Balanchine's *The Four Temperaments* (1990)

THE BOLENDER ERA

The goal had shifted, from creating a ballet company to putting it on the map. For this, a national search for an artistic director was launched. The challenge: convincing world-class talent to plant itself in middle America.

Meanwhile, volunteers stepped up to staff the company including Sarah Rowland as company manager. Elizabeth Wilson, new in town from the West Coast, had recently joined the Kansas City Ballet Board. "I certainly had no expertise," she recalled. "I didn't know anything about ballet, not a thing. And I didn't know anything about boards....I thought, if we're going to do this, let's try and do it right, just as you would do with an orchestra...or a Q-tip factory. Go and find out from the best people – first, is this viable, and second, do they know anyone whom you should talk to?"

A friend of Wilson's, Laurence Sickman, then director of the Nelson-Atkins Museum of Art, had gone to Harvard with the man responsible for bringing Balanchine to America: impresario Lincoln Kirstein. "So I picked up the phone and called him," said Wilson.

Kirstein's response: "I've got your man. You need to talk to Todd Bolender."

Born in 1914 in Canton, Ohio, Bolender was a Midwesterner himself, raised in an arts-friendly household. His mother was an amateur musician, his father a businessman. Early on, his energy and musicality found a home in dance class, a kind of "acrobatic tap."

Those local classes were the springboard for a global career that would span seven decades. At age sixteen, Todd drove trucks for the local parks department to earn enough money to study in New York. He won a scholarship with Edwin Strawbridge, his small budget fattened by a weekly five dollars from home for living expenses. Each summer for two years, the hazel-eyed teen returned to Ohio to drive trucks and save money for the next winter in New York. In 1933, he moved east for good, arriving in town about the same time as young George Balanchine.

It was a fertile time in the New York dance world. After seeing a concert by Mary Wigman, Bolender studied with Hanya Holm, a Wigman protégé and modern dance pioneer. Later he would count Wigman as one of his two greatest choreo-

13

Todd Bolender's marked-up score for *The Still Point*

graphic influences, along with India's renowned modern choreographer, Uday Shankar. When asked about his right turn into the ballet world, Bolender replied that during the Depression, he needed a job.

WHEN PATHS CROSS

He studied ballet with Chester Hale and Muriel Stuart (a pupil of Anna Pavlova and Louis Horst) and at Balanchine's School of American Ballet with Pierre Vladimiroff, Felia Doubrovska, Anatole Oboukhoff, and Ludmilla Schollar. As a student there, he met Lincoln Kirstein, the force who would twice alter the course of his life. In 1936, Kirstein gave Bolender his first job with Ballet Caravan under Balanchine's tutelage. More than forty years later, Kirstein would give him a second life-changing recommendation – to the Kansas City Ballet.

After Ballet Caravan closed, Bolender joined forces with William Dollar to form the American Concert Ballet, choreographing his first work in 1943 from nursery rhymes. *Mother Goose Suite*, a meditation on imagination and innocence, was set to Maurice Ravel's music by that title. In 1944, he danced with Ballet Theatre for four months before injuring himself, and in 1945 he joined Ballet Russe de Monte Carlo under the direction of George Balanchine.

THE BALANCHINE YEARS

The two worked together through every transmutation of Balanchine's companies. While directing Ballet Russe, Balanchine asked Bolender to join his new company, Ballet Society, which would later morph into the New York City Ballet (NYCB). As principal dancer, Bolender originated roles in some two dozen works of City Ballet's dazzling repertory – among them "Phlegmatic" in *The Four Temperaments*, "the Fox" in *Renard*, and "Sarabande" in *Agon*.

Jacques d'Amboise, lifelong compatriot and fellow principal with NYCB, would later say, "Do people realize that this man [Todd Bolender] created roles that no one else has ever been able to portray so well in dance – not I – not Villella – not anyone?"

Aside from his considerable charms as a performer, Bolender was interested in making dances from the outset of his career. He would work with Balanchine for some thirty years in the capacities of principal dancer and occasional choreographer, a duality that would continue through his last performance onstage at City Ballet's Stravinsky Festival in 1972, for which he created two pieces.

Although Balanchine allowed dancers to choreograph for the company, he could prove ambivalent when they did so. "I don't know if it was jealousy or what it was," reflected Bolender decades later in an interview, "but if he didn't like something you did, that was it." Balanchine cast a long shadow, and successive choreographers were often intimidated by it. "For me, there is no intimidation involved," said Bolender in an interview. "Balanchine simply opened a door, exposing a vast, vast horizon."

The view from Bolender's sixth-floor walk-up apartment kept expanding. Sally Brayley Bliss retells

Corinne Giddings, Susan Manchak, and Jody Anderson in Todd Bolender's *The Still Point* (1984)

one of Bolender's favorite stories: One day, Balanchine suggested that the young dancer entertain Igor Stravinsky and his wife that evening. Bolender made Herculean efforts to arrange his best menu in his modest home. After the winded Stravinskys arrived at the top of the stairs, hours passed in conversation until Bolender went to the kitchen to check on the food. In his nervousness, he had forgotten to turn on the oven! Fortunately, the Stravinskys had a working sense of humor.

CHOREOGRAPHING AND DIRECTING

Eventually Bolender left NYCB to direct ballet and opera ballet in America and Europe. Over a lifetime he choreographed thirty-six works for dozens of companies – including nine originally created for the New York City Ballet, and sixteen made especially for the Kansas City Ballet. His dances have been performed by most major companies, including American Ballet Theatre, Joffrey Ballet, San Francisco Ballet, Pacific Northwest Ballet, Alvin Ailey American Dance Theatre, and the opera houses of Cologne, Frankfurt, and Istanbul.

Like Balanchine, he also worked in musical theater, choreographing Broadway shows such as *Grand Hotel*, *Time Remembered*, *Rosalinda*, *New Faces*, and *The Conquering Hero*, and in Europe such perennials as *Kiss Me, Kate*, *My Fair Lady*, *Man of la Mancha*, and *Fiddler on the Roof.*

In 1980, he had just returned to New York from Istanbul when he got the call from America's heartland.

Bolender with
Kansas City Ballet sign,
1982

FIRST, A SCHOOL

Soon, board members were flying to New York and Bolender and Kirstein to Kansas City. After a proper interview, Bolender was offered the post. He accepted, with two conditions: first, the creation of a school, and second, live orchestral accompaniment for all performances.

Bolender rehearsing
with Ellen Makarewicz,
James Jordan, and
Helen Rosenthal (1981)

The dream of a school "was just in Todd's bones," says James Jordan, a charter member of Bolender's company who twenty-six years later serves as KCB's ballet master. "One of his greatest passions was developing talent. When he ran around the country putting his first company together, he wanted people he could train, not people who felt they were 'finished' and just wanted to learn ballets."

The transition was rough for some former KCB dancers whom Bolender did not hire. "People who didn't make it past the transition didn't 'get it,'" says Flo Klenklen, who performed under Dokoudovska for the better part of a decade. "Because it wasn't about what we could or couldn't do. It was about the next generation." Klenklen's tenure with Kansas City Ballet is the longest to date, spanning all its directors over thirty-six years, her role morphing from dancer to school administrator to teacher.

At age sixty-seven, the new director scoped out talent in New York, Los Angeles, and Kansas City, and at North Carolina School of the Arts, where Jordan was a student. "He kind of stunned people, because he didn't necessarily choose the stars of the class," Jordan recalls. "He picked four of us who were kind of scrappy, but he thought interesting." Bolender's travels yielded twenty dancers who joined three from KCB.

Bolender dug in and began to train and rehearse the new group. "These kids work very hard," he said in a 1981 inter-

Bolender's *Souvenirs* performed by Cathy Hazeltine and Robert Radford (1982)

Bolender and Una Kai, ballet mistress (1982)

view with *The Kansas City Star*. "Of course, they're young, and some are inexperienced stage-wise, but I don't mind a bit, because we're in the business of developing new dancers. That's what excited me about this whole venture."

CURTAIN UP

The new Kansas City Ballet debuted in a gala performance at the Music Hall on May 29, 1981. On the diverse program were two signature Bolender ballets, both created in 1955: *The Still Point*, a lyrical sextet inspired by the poetry of T. S. Eliot (originally set on a group of New York modern dancers), and the witty *Souvenirs*, a day-in-the-life of a swank hotel inhabited by a colorful cast of characters (originally created for NYCB). Rounding out the program was Balanchine's evergreen, *Pas de Dix*, and two pas de deux danced by guest artists Patricia McBride and Alexander Godunov.

At the end of the evening, the audience responded with a standing ovation, just the green light the troupe needed to move forward. Bolender turned to colleague Una Kai to become KCB's ballet mistress. They'd met at City Ballet in 1947, when she was in the corps and he was a principal, and had become famous friends. Kai had gone on to become ballet mistress, first at NYCB then at the Royal Danish Ballet, when Todd imported her to Kansas City. "I knew that

was going to be a good thing," she remembers, "and it was."

Although they shared equally the duties of teaching company class, Bolender credited Kai for having "given our dancers increasing polish" and technically advancing the troupe. Kai likewise gave Bolender credit: "Todd was such a wonderful teacher," she recalls. "All of us who trained with Balanchine adopted his ideas and his method, but Todd was the only one who constructed a class the way Balanchine did. There were no complicated combinations. Most of his combinations consisted of two steps. You just did them with various variations, at different speeds, and then with beats."

The first KCB works Bolender choreographed were *Classical Symphony* and *Tchaikovsky Suite*, the latter with students from the newly formed school. But his first full-length ballet for the company would establish one of the region's most cherished holiday traditions: *Nutcracker* premiered in 1981 to capacity crowds.

In the decades to follow, Bolender continued to reinvent *Nutcracker*, editing and devising new costumes and sets. For "Waltz of the Flowers," few would guess how he pinned fabric swatches on the dancers to track a color palette through six trios' shifting patterns. Using this color-coded geometry, he was able to create a kinetic painting, a synesthesia borne of music, motion, and hue that blurs and blooms into sudden visual harmonies. *Nutcracker* continues to fulfill another Bolender mission, bringing talent from the Kansas City Ballet School shoulder to shoulder with the company. Today with 25 professionals and some 200 students rotating through multiple casts, the massive production accounts for 592 pointe shoes, one

Bolender's *Nutcracker* featuring local actor Cain DeVore as Drosselmeyer with students from the Kansas City Ballet School (1981)

flying sleigh, and uncountable snowflakes.

By 1982, the troupe was ready to take on more of Balanchine's work, and Bolender created a festival to honor his mentor of some thirty years. He selected four early ballets that "Balanchine did for the New York City Ballet when it was a young company, and that we are capable of doing as a young company": *Serenade, À la Françaix, Valse Fantaisie*, and *Firebird*, and imported guest artists Maria Terezia Balogh and Michael Dwyer. *Serenade*, Balanchine's first creation after coming to America, had made a believer of Bolender when he saw it at age twenty-one. "I was absolutely bowled over," he remembered. "I said to myself, This is what dancing is all about."

Luminaries flew to Kansas City for the Balanchine Festival, including former NYCB ballerina Maria Tallchief and Lincoln Kirstein, without whom America would not have had Balanchine and Kansas City would not have had Bolender. Invitations for the kickoff party stated, "Dress: Sensational!" and boas, beads, and berets ruled the evening. The reviews were sensational as well. *Ballet News* noted KCB's "joyous exuberance, keen dramatic sense, and zest for movement," and declared the company reborn "on a fast track, bringing taste, technique and an ineffable sense of quality to the heartland."

THE REHEARSAL PROCESS

Bolender was a protégé of Balanchine, but not a mimic. Like Balanchine, he pushed the body conspicuously beyond a dancerly range of motion and draped whole ballets on the skeleton of the music, but Bolender's offbeat wit and theatricality were all his own. *Dance Magazine* said, "His humor is not an inside joke but a sudden playful abandon, a tongue-in-

cheek poke at his own seriousness. He makes clear, uncluttered statements....Then he cleanses the stage with group movements."

While often his dances revealed his wit, rehearsals were serious business. "He certainly couldn't stand any sort of levity in the studio if he was concentrating," said James Jordan, who would eventually succeed Una Kai. "He would be annoyed if someone cracked their knuckles. He just wanted silence." Bolender would arrive in his workday "uniform" – signature turtleneck, flowing overshirt, cotton trousers, and jazz shoes – with score in hand.

"He was very mathematical in his approach," remembers Francisco Renno, company pianist from 1981 to 1999, who readied Bolender for rehearsal by breaking down the score into dance-friendly counts. "He would put the score on the floor and hunch over it from his chair. There would be thirty-minute pauses where he would do nothing but stare at the score. There had to be complete silence: You couldn't talk; you couldn't cough. Then he would rise and make up something. Sometimes we would be in the studio for six hours and do eight measures!"

"Musicality is the basis of everything," Bolender declared in a *New York Times* interview. In an interview with the *St. Louis Globe-Democrat*, he said, "What's important is that the articulations were rhythmically precise, for it's through unified response to the music, not through automaton-like imagery, that a dance's energy is best projected." Early on, he was able to convey this philosophy to his dancers. A *St. Louis Post-Dispatch* review of Bolender's *Nutcracker* noted, "The musicality of the dancers in general is impressive. Indeed, collective musicality is probably the main thing that gives this company an edge over most of the Midwest's other professional troupes."

When asked what most stayed with him about Todd Bolender, Jordan hesitated, gazed into his lap, and replied simply: "Music." During rehearsals, "Todd would just clear his throat or do a subtle little grunt if someone was the least bit 'off.' I couldn't slip anything by him. It had to be just right. We developed all these counting systems so that there would be no room for error."

Furthermore, he never allowed dancers to "mark" (indicate

Rendering by set designer Robert Fletcher
of *Nutcracker* battle scene (1994)

PHOTO BY KEVIN MANNING, *ST. LOUIS POST-DISPATCH*

Bolender with Deena Budd during a
Nutcracker rehearsal in St. Louis (1996)

their steps without actually dancing them). "In the studio," Bolender remarked, "you must learn how to breathe, how much you can do, how much energy is required. If you've never danced a piece full-out, you're at the mercy of your nerves when you're onstage." Jordan remembers the no-marking philosophy as "all work and no play. Todd thought [marking] was just a waste of his time and ours. We were young, and we needed to get better, and we wouldn't get the least bit better if we marked."

REGIONAL EXPANSION

By the 1983-84 season, Kansas City Ballet was ready to hit the road, doubling its performance season with twenty-five tour dates in five states: Missouri, Kansas, Arkansas, Nebraska, and Wyoming. "Many in the company were virtually unfamiliar with the Midwest outside of Kansas City," said then Company Manager Kevin Amey (now general manager in his twenty-fifth year with KCB). Some dancers from New York and California had never seen a cornfield. "Rolling around through the wilds of Arkansas on a bus was quite an experience," Amey continued. "The terrain was accentuated on a bus," and winding, rolling highways translated to motion sickness for the poets-in-motion.

While the audience response was "always terrific," according to Amey, critical acclaim followed. "This is one of the most dynamic companies in the Midwest," declared the *St. Louis Post-Dispatch*, "and something ought to be done to make their visits to St. Louis more than just an annual occurrence."

Something would be done. In 1986, in a joint venture with Dance St. Louis, the board announced that the Kansas City Ballet would henceforth become the "State Ballet of Missouri." Then General Manager Michael Kaiser, now president of

the John F. Kennedy Center for the Performing Arts, facilitated the deal: "The idea was, if we could really build up the relationship in St. Louis, then we would have an opportunity to virtually double the season in Kansas City just with those two cities alone," offering increased exposure while expanding the fund-raising base.

Both locally and regionally, stellar reviews became the norm. "The State Ballet is one of the finest classical ballet companies in the country right now," raved *The Kansas City Star*. From the *St. Louis Post-Dispatch:* "The State Ballet of Missouri proved without a doubt last weekend why it is one of the brightest gems in the state's crown jewels and is fast becoming a topic on the national scene."

Amid the flying superlatives, Bolender was sparing in his praise, always asking his dancers for more than they thought they could give. He asked no less of himself. From the outset of his directorship, he had planned to choreograph George Gershwin's exhilarating "Piano Concerto in F" for the company. "I thought it would be the perfect music for a company-building ballet," he said. "The variety in it calls for many different kinds of steps, different kinds of movement, different feelings."

PHOTO BY STRAUSS-PEYTON INC.

In costume for Balanchine's *Concerto Barocco* at the St. Louis Arch, Alecia Good, Laurinda Mackay, Gretchen Klockë, and Douglass Stewart (1991)

Its slow but steady construction would span several years. He premiered the first movement in 1983 and got the second and third movements on their feet in 1984. *The Kansas City Star* called Bolender's *Concerto in F* a "perfect tonic...Every note of George Gershwin's score is like champagne, as is every step."

SCHOOL DAYS

Meanwhile, the Kansas City Ballet School (KCBS) was well under way. "Todd and Una, how they worked when they first came here!" recalls Flo Klenklen, the school administrator. "They alternated teaching company class, they'd rehearse all day long, and then they both came back to teach in the school at night. It was extraordinary. They loved the school."

As punctuation, guest teachers were invited to augment the regular faculty and fire up the students. Notables such as Judith Jamison, Jacques d'Amboise, Allegra Kent, Janet Reed, Sandra Jennings, Rosella Hightower, and Mireille Briane would be in residence for two weeks to a month, or over a summer.

In 1983, following Jonathan Watts's tenure, Bolender recruited Diana Adams (former principal with both New York City Ballet and American Ballet Theatre) to head the KCBS staff and focus its pedagogical philosophy. "When Diana Adams came in, the world changed," Klenklen continues. "Diana knew more about Balanchine training than anyone, because she was the original teacher that Balanchine trained to direct the School of American Ballet."

Adams's syllabus became something of a roadmap which successors Vicki Fedine, then Lisa Dillinger and Klenklen would set out in greater detail, providing continuity from teacher to teacher. Following this syllabus, the school was able to offer a seamless experience for its students as they moved through the ranks.

One of those students was eleven-year-old Christopher Barksdale, who began his training in 1982. "I remember the first day of class with Christopher," says Klenklen, chuckling. "He didn't understand that he needed to stay at the barre, and he followed me all around the room. 'No, no, Chris, you've got to stay at the barre. Put your hand on the barre.'"

Klenklen remembers one day when Bolender was rehearsing the Chinese section of *Nutcracker*: "Chris marched up to Todd and said, 'I'm gonna be doing that one of these days. That's the role I'm gonna do.' Todd said, 'Yes, dear, yes, dear.'" Christopher Barksdale fulfilled not only his own dream, but the dream of the school to grow its own dancers. In a half-dozen years, he would perform the coveted Chinese Dance, and twenty-four years later, he is still dazzling audiences. Eight dancers from KCBS went on to become company members.

THE BIG APPLE

Within five years of Todd Bolender's arrival, Kansas City Ballet had built a school and a repertoire, become an acclaimed regional presence, and changed its name. By 1987, it was ready for the big time – New York. For the debut, KCB mounted four Bolender ballets – two older, *Souvenirs* and *The Still Point*, and two newer, *Classical Symphony* and *Concerto in F*.

Much was at stake. Bolender, Kai, and the dancers had flocks of colleagues in New York, and "We wanted to make an impression," said Kai. "We thought that we brought the best program that we were able to do at that time, and dancers who were certainly top-notch – a lot of them trained by us."

Appearing at the Brooklyn Center for the Performing Arts, the company garnered fine reviews from the New York and national press. Francis Mason of WQXR, the radio station of *The New York Times*, had this to say: "Ballet from Kansas City had New York cheering last weekend....The State Ballet of Missouri dances rings around most of the imports we have from Europe, and makes it clearer than ever that ballet in America is the best in the world....The Missouri dancers were graced with superb inner rhythm and abundant but controlled energy....ballet at its best. This company is smart, handsome, and right on the mark."

MONEY MATTERS

Not only had Kansas City Ballet made it to New York, but along the way it brought New York (and London) to Kansas City. During the Bolender days,

Todd Bolender, Muriel McBrien Kauffman, and Board President Tom Johnston (1990)

Revival of Balanchine's *Renard* at 2001 Stravinski Festival with Paris Wilcox, Sean Duus, Christopher Barksdale, and Anthony Krutzkamp

the company occasionally functioned as a presenting organization, importing big-name dance (Mikhail Baryshnikov and Twyla Tharp) to the community and dollars to KCB's budget. In 1988, Rudolf Nureyev and Friends came to town under its wing, generating some $160,000 in earned income. The strategy lifted all KCB's boats: season ticket sales increased 21 percent; earned income jumped 36 percent; the annual Ballet Ball netted $132,500.

Bolender, whose passion was making dances, found himself spending at least as much time raising money and expanding audiences. "It's getting tighter and tighter all the time, with administrative duties, to find time to choreograph new ballets," he said in a 1989 *Star* interview. In 1993, KCB was invited into the National Arts Stabilization Fund program, a five-year debt-reduction and institutional enhancement program. Through NASF and then General Manager Martin Cohen's leadership, the company successfully met rigorous benchmarks, eliminated its deficit, and established a capital reserve. Kansas City's foundations and families rallied, and longtime friend of the arts Muriel Kauffman, board chairman

1990-92, was especially kind to the ballet. Among her many gestures was the 1994 endowment of $1 million for Kansas City Ballet (one of four area arts organizations to receive such an honor).

"My mother loved to dance, period," says daughter Julia Irene Kauffman. But her favorite partner on the dance floor was Todd Bolender. "Todd said, 'I always tried to trip her up, but I never could.'" After her death, Bolender choreographed a ballet in her honor, *Tribute to Muriel*.

Muriel McBrien Kauffman's generosity was pivotal to the life of the company, and after her passing has been graciously carried on by Julia Irene Kauffman, chairman of the Kansas City Ballet Board since 1999. "My mission has been to follow her mission, and her love of the performing arts," she said recently. "I'm out to make my mother's mission come true."

WIT, WISDOM, AND REPERTOIRE

For a boy who never graduated from high school, Todd Bolender was a man of ideas. "When you go to the ballet, you're not to go and sit as if you're in a warm bath," he asserted. A self-educated world traveler, he was a voracious reader who devoured historical nonfiction and *The New York Times*, and loved spending long afternoons at the Nelson-Atkins Museum of Art.

"Through the depth of his education, Todd acquired good taste, and it rubbed off on everybody," recalls James Jordan. That would include Jordan himself, whom Bolender handpicked as the official stager of his ballets. In a *Dance*

Bolender with acclaimed sculptor and designer Dale Eldred before the performance of *Voyager*, one of several collaborations between Bolender and Eldred (1984)

Magazine interview, Bolender hailed Jordan's "intelligence and intuition," noting that "as a stager he has an extraordinary facility to make the thing as it was originally."

History was made when KCB reconstructed two of Balanchine's "lost ballets" choreographed in 1947. Unperformed for decades and never videotaped or set in notation, the dances were lovingly resurrected, step by step, out of the bodies that had originally danced them. Bolender enlisted Francisco Moncion and Tanaquil LeClercq to help reconstruct *Divertimento* in 1985. Moncion, who had danced with Bolender in the first cast, recalled in an interview, "It was strictly in my head....I'd say that the ballet is 95 percent authentic," adding that he filled in memory gaps with vocabulary from the piece.

Later, Bolender with Jordan would recreate the lost *Renard*, its comic misadventures involving a fox, ram, rooster, and cat. Bolender had played the original Fox, and the painstaking three-year archival reconstruction was accomplished at the behest of the George Balanchine Foundation and taped by the Foundation's Archive of Lost Choreography. Invited to New York to perform *Renard* at Symphony Space for the "Wall to Wall Balanchine" tribute, KCB "hit the stage running" and was declared a "highlight" of the festival by *Dance Magazine*.

On the whole, the company's repertoire was dominated by Balanchine and Bolender, but reflected such diverse sensibilities as Antony Tudor, Jerome Robbins, August Bournonville, Jacques d'Amboise, and Marius Petipa. From storied ballets to plotless neoclassical pieces, the tone varied from light to satirical to dramatic to dark. Reflecting Bolender's early penchant for modern dance, three pieces by long-time friend Alvin Ailey were acquired, taking the dancers' speedy airborne technique in new directions that emphasized the spine, pelvis, and floor, in what the *Star* called "a new elastic, sinewy, taut dance style."

Donna Wood, Alvin Ailey, and Todd Bolender (1986)

Bolender's own foray into modern dance was *Voyager*, a 1984 collaboration with internationally acclaimed Kansas City sculptor Dale Eldred to music by Leonard Bernstein. This was Bolender's most ambitious piece and the one he considered his most important. Using projected images from NASA's 1979 Voyager mission, Eldred strove to recreate deep space within a theatrical context. Amid this interplanetary environment, Bolender traced the development of humanity from the "star soup" of the universe. It was a lofty project, launching a Bolender/Eldred partnership that continued for four ballets over a half-dozen years (*Voyager, Danse Concertante, An American in Paris,* and *Celebration*).

In 1995, at age eighty-one, Bolender retired from artistic directorship to assume an emeritus role. In fifteen years he had taken the company from its Midwestern nest to a national platform. Operating on a $2.5 million annual budget, the company now boasted 27 dancers performing a diverse repertoire, and a school of 150 students. In short, Bolender had taught Kansas City Ballet how to fly. An international search began for the person who could guide the company into the future.

Freed from his duties as director, Bolender could focus on what he loved most: collaborating with like-minded artists. The last piece he choreographed at age eighty-two was *Arena*, commissioned by a "Meet the Composer" grant with James Mobberley, composition professor at the UMKC Conservatory and composer-in-residence with the Kansas City Symphony. *Arena* premiered in the fall of 1996, an ambient twenty-two minutes enveloping the history of human folly and sorrow in a birthing/mourning scenario by a black-swathed Mother Earth. Featuring a politician on stilts and a luscious

21

nocturnal backdrop by Russell Ferguson, the ballet was hailed by *The Kansas City Star* as "gripping....Rich and strange, it's a work fairly bristling with invention."

Todd Bolender credited exercise for his longevity. Still active with KCB at the age of ninety-two, he learned he was to be given the Dance Magazine Award for his lifelong contribution to the art. On October 12, 2006, he died unexpectedly after suffering a stroke. He had spent the previous weekend in the studio coaching the cast of his *Grand Tarantella*. Days earlier, he appeared at the groundbreaking for the Kauffman Center for the Performing Arts, where dancers performed an excerpt from his signature work, *The Still Point*.

Five hundred people gathered from around the country to attend his memorial service at the Music Hall. Jacques d'Amboise returned to the stage he'd danced on in KCB's early days to pay tribute: "[Todd Bolender's] genius was in giving full value to every simple gesture or movement of the dance, as if it were the only movement he would ever make, the beginning and the end of the universe."

Perhaps the most telling tribute to the nonagenarian is the loyalty and longevity of those who worked with him. Eight dancers from the Bolender era still work with the company in some capacity. Two dancers from the Dokoudovska era served in decades-long staff roles. "What I feel happiest about," said former ballet mistress Una Kai, "is that we took dancers who stayed with us the entire time. We had a group who became really fine dancers, and I've always felt very proud." One was twenty-six-year veteran James Jordan, whose poignant tribute capped the memorial service. Having given each person in the audience a red rose, he led the crowd in a dancerly salute, raising a veritable field of roses to one who loved flowers.

In 2009, the Kansas City Ballet will move into its permanent new home, the Todd Bolender Center for Dance and Creativity. But his legacy lives most visibly in the company he disappeared into – in their athleticism, their musicality, and their remarkable ability to trade earth for air. ∎

Todd Bolender with Aisling Hill-Connor at *Nutcracker* rehearsal (2005)

Company photo 1991.

Bottom row, seated: Oliver Kovach, Eve Lawson, Jody Anderson, Sean Duus

First row: Kendall Klym, Trina Yatsko, Kathleen Berry, Maura McKenna, William Dunne, Douglass Stewart, Michael Koetting, Robert Skafte, Susan Manchak

Second row: Pamela Ford, James Jordan, Louise Nadeau, Susan Lewis, Brian Staihr, Alecia Good, Gretchen Klockë, Goddard Finley

On windowsill: Deena Budd, Daniel Catanach, Michel DeVeers, Maura Montgomery

Architect's rendering by BNIM of the new Todd Bolender Center for Dance and Creativity

23

Russell Baker and members of the Kansas City Ballet perform *Arena*, a collaboration of composer James Mobberley and choreographer Todd Bolender (1996)

Scott Alan Barker in Balanchine's *Prodigal Son* (1990)

Christopher Barksdale in Bolender's collaboration with designer Dale Eldred, *Danse Concertante* (2005)

Todd Bolender with Julia Irene Kauffman before the groundbreaking ceremony for the Kauffman Center for the Performing Arts (2006)

Guillermo Ramirez, Sean Duus, Alecia Good,
Andrew Kallem, and Scott Alan Barker in
Bolender's *Coppelia* (1993)

Alecia Good in
Bolender's *Coppelia* (1993)

Lauren Wright, Laurinda Mackay,
and Deena Budd in Bolender's
Grand Tarantella (1991)

25

Laurinda Mackay and Robert Skafte in *Nutcracker* snow costumes in the living room of Muriel Kauffman (1991)

PHOTO BY STRAUSS-PEYTON INC.

PHOTOS BY DON MIDDLETON

Bolender's *The Miraculous Mandarin* with Jody Anderson and James Jordan (1985)

Louise Nadeau and Brian Staihr in Balanchine's *Raymonda Variations* (1989)

Louise Nadeau and
Brian Staihr in Bolender's
An American in Paris (1987)

Alvin Ailey's *The River* featuring Jody Anderson (1986)

Brian Staihr and Eve Lawson with pianist Francisco
Renno in Bolender's *Chopin Piano Pieces* (1986)

Kimberly Cowen in *Carmen* (2007)

THREE

THE
WHITENER
ERA

The letter went out: "On February 1, 1995, the Board of Directors of the State Ballet of Missouri announced the opening of an international search for our new Artistic Director....We are seeking an individual who brings a broad range of talent and who can build on the solid foundation established by Todd Bolender."

While board members were initially seeking someone of Balanchine lineage, their search eventually led to a leader with more eclectic roots: William Whitener. "He had such an impressive resume," says Wendy Powell, former board president who chaired the search committee. "I knew right away that there was an appreciation for the ethos at New York City Ballet if [Whitener] had been staging works for Jerome Robbins."

William Whitener offered a diversity of experience as a dancer, choreographer, and director. A veteran dancer with both the Joffrey Ballet and Twyla Tharp Dance, he had performed internationally, choreographed extensively, appeared on Broadway, film, and television, and directed two quite different Canadian entities: Les Ballets Jazz de Montreal and the Royal Winnipeg Ballet.

Whitener flew out for the interview, taught company class, and confirmed the best hopes of the committee. "He's personable, he's outgoing, he's respectful of the dancers," Powell remembers thinking. "You can tell a lot by watching somebody teach class. I felt I was seeing the scope of his talent."

EARLY SIGNS

The depth and diversity of William Whitener's career was the natural result of an immersion in the arts from childhood onward. Born in 1951 in Seattle, he was the elder of two children from parents raised in farming communities. His father would eventually become a salesman, and his mother an entrepreneur who ran her own handiwork business.

Whitener credits his mother's perpetual creativity as his door into the arts. "You see a project from start to finish, so that a ball of yarn becomes a sweater." At the age of seven, he began ballet training as an outlet for his tremendous energy. After school, he would dance and improvise for hours. "I'd push the furniture aside, then go up and jump off the couch."

Along the way he added figure skating, piano, and oboe to his studies while also performing as an actor and singer. He took summer courses with the Joffrey Ballet at a nearby college and at age seventeen was awarded a scholarship to its professional school in New York. He graduated from high school early, and within three months of moving was offered a job with the Joffrey Ballet.

JOFFREY, THARP, AND BEYOND

"You could live alone in 1969 in New York on a salary of $95," Whitener remembers of his early days in the Joffrey. His studio apartment in Soho had a twin bed, table and chairs, and a "kitchenette-*ette.*" That first year he worked with a man who would loom large in his life a quarter-century later: Todd Bolender. In 1970, Bolender was setting two ballets on the Joffrey and "created an environment that made me think I could excel," Whitener recalls.

From his postage-stamp apartment, the world unrolled as Whitener performed throughout the United States as well as in Canada, Europe, Russia, and the Far East. He danced a range of principal roles, interpreting the highly dissimilar work of George Balanchine, Gerald Arpino, Kurt Jooss, Jerome Robbins, Margo Sappington, Anna Sokolow, and Alvin Ailey – and an upstart named Twyla Tharp.

In 1973, Tharp was invited to set a ballet on the Joffrey. *Deuce Coupe* inserted modern dancers among pointe-shoed ballerinas in an admixture of sliding, skipping, and slinking punctuated by that era's popular dance moves – the jerk, frug, and monkey. The ballet dancers revolted. After three weeks of rehearsal, Tharp delivered an ultimatum: If you don't want to be here, leave. Three-quarters of the Joffrey walked; William Whitener stayed. At twenty-one, he was thirsty for such an influence, relishing Tharp's visceral experi-

ments in improvisation and problem-solving.

Meanwhile his own love of making dances sought an outlet. "I asked Robert Joffrey and Sally Bliss (then director of the junior company) for a chance to create a new work there, and they said yes," Whitener recalls. The result was *Boomfallera*, choreographed on Joffrey II, which enjoyed high visibility and put Whitener on the path as a choreographer in 1976.

Whitener joined the original Broadway cast of Bob Fosse's *Dancin'* in 1978, and later that year became a leading dancer with Twyla Tharp Dance, where he would stay nearly nine years. "I just listened to her and tried to do what she wanted," he says laughing, when asked about working with the some-times difficult Tharp. "I thought that her requests and her expectations were fascinating, so there was no reason not to try. Oftentimes the requests were basically impossible, but the *attempt* at the impossible became the choreography."

In particular, he remembers the "accidents" in rehearsal that were not threatening. "We were trying things that were so difficult that they would produce an 'accident.' Then we would try to reproduce that....take it apart and figure what actually happened. It would be a group tumble, a missing piece of physical support...that then created a different kind of movement or action."

Whitener toured the world with Tharp's company, performing for President Reagan at the White House and appearing in the film *Amadeus* as well as on PBS, ABC, and the BBC. After retiring in 1987, he went on to assist Jerome Robbins with reconstruction and staging for *Robbins' Broadway* and toured with Martha Clarke's *The Garden of Earthly Delights*. In 1989, after two decades in New York, Whitener left the city to begin a freelance adventure that would take him to Canada via Seattle.

Ultimately he choreographed for theater, opera, ballroom dancers, even skaters (including Olympic gold medalist John Curry), as well as for dance companies including the Boston Ballet, the Royal Winnipeg Ballet, Pacific Northwest Ballet, Les Ballets Jazz de Montreal, Ballet Hispanico, Hartford Ballet, Joffrey II, and the Princeton Ballet. He made pieces for artists as dissimilar as Ann Reinking, Martine van Hamel, Tommy Tune, and Kevin McKenzie.

In 1991, he headed to Canada to direct Les Ballets Jazz de Montreal, accepting an offer in 1993 to become artistic director of the Royal Winnipeg Ballet. As one of four directors funneled through that troupe in eight years, Whitener stayed for two. "The chemistry wasn't right," he said. Ironically, it was in Winnipeg that Whitener and current KCB Executive Director Jeffrey Bentley first met. Bentley had taken the executive directorship in Winnipeg just as the previous artistic director was exiting and was instrumental in encouraging the search committee to hire Whitener as its new artistic leader.

In 1995, Whitener heard about the opening with Kansas City Ballet. "I did my homework and had a look at the repertory," he said in an interview with the *Star*. "I started to talk with various people...about the vision – what's needed, what exists, what's been founded by Mr. Bolender, the dreams."

Goin' to Kansas City

For Whitener, the lure was threefold: Artistic Director Emeritus Todd Bolender, the company itself, and the city behind the company. "There was such a kinship between William and Todd right off the bat," remembers Search Committee Chair Wendy Powell.

"This is the man that I felt really had it," Bolender said of Whitener in a 1996 interview for *Pitch Weekly*. "He's very bright...and really knows what dance is all about and all the elements that make it."

Whitener felt the company was "marvelous" and the city compelling. In the fall of 1996, his life started over. "I took one highway from Winnipeg to Kansas City," he said in an interview with *Kansas City Magazine*. "I put my foot on the gas and barely had to make a turn."

Let the Wild Rumpus Start

The challenges were many and immediate. Not only did Whitener have to emerge from Bolender's long shadow, but he had to do so amid a series of retrenchments. The first pointe shoe to drop: Dance St. Louis decided to terminate its ten-year, two-city relationship with Kansas City Ballet after the 1996-97 season. The second, third, and fourth: KCB's own budget cuts necessitated a reduction of its season from three repertory programs to two, the temporary replacement of live music with recorded music, and a cutback in dancers – a third of whom had resigned in the turnover.

"It *is* a turnover," said Whitener in a *Star* interview. "But it's probably not much different from what I'm hearing from across the country. It's not uncommon when you have a change of artistic directors for people who may have been thinking of moving on or retiring to feel able to make that decision."

In the Wings

Whitener went about making lemonade from lemons. He found a low-cost but priceless solution that resurrected the three-program season and would become a company staple. Drawing on his experience choreographing at Joffrey, Whitener established "In the Wings" to give company members a chance to explore ideas choreographically. Experimenting with their gifted peers, dancers rehearse for six weeks – three in October alongside *Nutcracker* preparations, three in March – and debut their work in public performances with discussion and feedback.

"It gives [dancers] a chance to collaborate with their colleagues and direct each other," said Whitener. "They can see how it works from the other side, from the creative rather than the interpretive." Thus the workshop trains more than composition and directing skills. Dancers gain patience and compassion for guest choreographers who face the inevitable difficulties of creating new work.

Let the Music Play

Whitener's goal of diversifying Kansas City Ballet's repertoire began as talk: "The repertory will expand under my leadership, and we will be presenting a very wide spectrum of dance," he said in an interview with the Missouri Arts Council. "The artists will be required to stretch and learn some new techniques and styles of dance to which they might not yet have been exposed."

Lisa Thorn in Agnes de Mille's *Rodeo* (1996)

First, Whitener strove to reinforce the foundation from which to diverge. His debut program in the fall of 1996 smartly blended a revival of George Balanchine's *Scotch Symphony*, Agnes de Mille's classic *Rodeo*, and Todd Bolender's last work, *Arena*. Come spring of 1997, Whitener contributed a piece of his own, *The Scarlatti Dances*, celebratory in tone while being comfortably reminiscent of the neoclassical tradition so familiar to Kansas City balletomanes. *The Star* raved: "Singly, in pairs, trios, quartets, and quintets, occasionally with a soloist counterpointing the ensemble, the dancers go through the most graceful geometries, ending with a wonderfully lacy ensemble....It's a gracious ballet, and the company looks fabulous dancing it."

The next season, live music for all programs was resurrected, and the Ballet was thrilled to have Kansas City Symphony members back in the orchestra pit – a longstanding partnership of excellence envisioned from the outset. With the orchestra securely in place, music was raised to a conspicuous new level. Whitener's *A Midsummer Night's Dream* to Felix Mendelssohn's "peerless score" featured members of the Kansas City Chorale out front, and was hailed by the *Star* as "ballet at its best." A revival of Paula Weber's *Carmina Burana* to Carl Orff's pulsating music climaxed in its triangulation of the orchestra in the pit, the symphony chorus at the right of the house, and the company swirling across the stage.

In 1999, two world premieres also elevated live music from the audible to the visible. Former Paul Taylor dancer Lila York's *Gloria* situated the Kansas City Symphony Chorus out front with the Kansas City Symphony Ballet Orchestra in the pit, rendering the lush music of Francis Poulenc. In *Suite Kander*, Tony Award-winning Ann Reinking placed a six-musician band right alongside the dancers. Her Fosse-esque rendition of John Kander's music brought the stage to a sizzle and the audience to its feet screaming and whistling. "Sensational jazz at its best," raved the *Star*. "The dancers look like they're having a blast on stage."

Almost imperceptibly, the *Queen Mary* was being turned. A sea change was coming.

COMING HOME

In January 2000, the Kansas City Ballet officially reclaimed its original name, having performed as the State Ballet of Missouri for nearly fifteen years. Returning to the designation of its founder Tatiana Dokoudovska in 1957, the company had come full circle – spiritually to its artistic origins and geographically to Kansas City. In so doing, both the company and the city acknowledged their importance to each other.

While "In the Wings" developed resources within the company, outreach programs poured them back into the community. The signature in-school program, "Reach Out and Dance" (ROAD), was inspired by Jacques d'Amboise's National Dance Institute. Established by Director of Community Programs Linda Martin, ROAD introduces eight hundred grade-schoolers a year to dance fundamentals while addressing education standards. Remarkably but not surprisingly, participants show improvement in self-discipline, concentration, and academic achievement – and they love ROAD, which reaches every fourth-grader in eleven schools for one hour each week.

"Ballet in the Park" brings free annual dance concerts in parks across the area to thousands who might not otherwise be exposed to the art. Whitener offers "Footnotes," an informal talk, one hour before every performance to help build a bridge from the stage to the audience.

32

PHOTOS BY STEVE WILSON

Whitener's *A Midsummer Night's Dream* with Kimberly Cowen, Russell Baker, and Christopher Barksdale (2002)

Ann Reinking's *Suite Kander* (1999)

A GALLERY OF DANCE

That bridge is crucial to the growth of the company. By diversifying the repertoire, Whitener has concurrently diversified its audience. "How moved I am when I go to the ballet and hardly know anyone in the audience!" says veteran supporter Wendy Powell, who has served under every director.

Whitener likes addressing the public's "fear of ballet.... It really isn't so different than going to see artwork in a gallery," he says. "You won't like everything you see, but there's bound to be something to pique your interest and will make you want to come back for more."

His next piece would explore another wing of the gallery – ballroom dance. Co-choreographed with Tharp colleague Shelley Freydont, *On the Boulevard* premiered in October 2000, offering a thirty-minute pastiche of fox trot, tango, bolero, quickstep, waltz, swing, jive, and blues. As in other recent ventures, dancers shared the stage with musicians (Boulevard Big Band and vocalist Karrin Allyson). "The performance ripped through the notion of ballet as an art form for fragile nymphs in tutus," said the *Star* review.

Moving from Fred and Ginger to the twelve-tone scale, the company joined in the 2001 Stravinsky Festival with an all-Balanchine program showcasing his quintessential design masterpiece, *Agon*. Created in 1957, the complex ballet was set on KCB by Patricia Neary, formerly of City Ballet. "You have to count through a lot of the work without moving your lips," said Neary referring to the atonal score that jags through different time signatures every few measures. The result was KCB's "most glorious moment to date," according to an *Arts News* critic. "The dancing was impeccable....Technically, all the dancers were thoroughbreds."

In 2002, Whitener paid tribute to Robert Joffrey with a program choreographed by Joffrey veterans. He commissioned colleagues Margo Sappington and Marjorie Mussman to create new ballets, alongside a return of his own *The Scarlatti Dances*. The dances were utterly unalike, and the juxtaposition stunning. Following the Whitener revival, Mussman's *The Chariot* used the evocative music of Aaron Copland to illuminate Emily Dickinson's poetry. In another universe, Sappington's *ZuZu Lounge* combined "bachelor-pad" music by Juan Garcia Esquivel, insect-like Christian Holder costumes, and space-age lighting to create a truly odd and witty semblance of an underground cocktail party.

Paris Wilcox and Aisling Hill-Connor in Balanchine's *Agon* (2001)

Lisa Thorn and Russell Baker with jazz vocalist Karrin Allyson in Whitener and Freydont's *On the Boulevard* (2000)

33

Margo Sappington's
ZuZu Lounge (2002)

William Whitener's "real strength is in his programming, his ability to put an interesting evening together," says Powell, who serves on KCB's Advisory Council and on the National Advisory Council for NYCB's School of American Ballet. Whitener's recipe: crowd-pleasing appetizer, nutritious main course, flambé finish. Here Joffrey's influence is hard to miss. "Joffrey didn't create the triple bill," wrote *Dance Magazine*, "...but he brought excitement, novelty, sexiness, and diversity to the concept."

In the spring of 2002, Whitener gathered solos from six mavericks (Lotte Goslar, Anna Sokolow, Merce Cunningham, Agnes de Mille, Daniel Nagrin, and Michel Fokine) into one overarching piece, *Six Solos*. The result garnered national attention. *Six Solos* was featured in *The New York Times* and earned the cover story of *Dance Magazine*. Paul Horsley of the *Star* called it "quite simply one of the most exciting evenings I've spent in this city." The project was so successful that it spawned a sequel in 2006, *Six Solos of Consequence II*. Remarkably, the second version outshone the first, featuring choreography by such strange bedfellows as Claire Porter (with spoken word), Isadora Duncan, Mary Wigman, George Balanchine (in two pieces), and Bob Fosse.

In 2003, Kansas City Ballet honored the fiftieth anniversary of the Merce Cunningham Dance Company by performing his work. *Duets* was staged by Catherine Kerr, Cunningham's original partner, using the same methodology Cunningham had used to create the piece. Dancers rehearsed in silence with a stopwatch, then switched to John Cage's music only after they had mastered the split-second timing.

On that same program was the world premiere of *Haven*, Whitener's response to 9/11 with music by Toru Takemitsu. Perforated hanging panels by artist Jason Pollen, dramatic lighting by Kirk Book-man, and Whitener's spare choreography combined to suggest the Twin Towers transforming into a temple, death into resurrection. "It was a bold and striking departure..." raved the *Star*, "atmospheric, savage, and refreshingly unbusy."

The following fall, a full-length *Giselle* by Jules Perrot and Jean Coralli reaffirmed the troupe's "strength in the classics." From the *Star* review: "The Kansas City Ballet has grown into such a versatile company that we sometimes forget the extent of its achievements in the very style it purports to espouse: ballet."

From the dramatic *Giselle* to Jerome Robbins's comedic *The Concert*, Kansas City Ballet continued to take big risks and land on its capable feet. If, as the saying goes, death is easy and comedy hard, the company was getting plenty of practice – from the witty dance monologues of Claire Porter to the bizarre undertones of *ZuZu Lounge* to the coffin antics of Ruth Page's *Frankie and Johnny* to the unpredictable bursts of humor in Lynne Taylor-Corbett's *Great Gallop-ing Gottschalk*. "The time is ripe for the return of the comic ballet," said Whitener. "People want to laugh in the theater. It's one of the reasons we go." When NYCB veteran Bart Cook set Robbins's *The Concert* on KCB dancers in 2004, he "warned them about how much laughter there would be. And sure enough, it did throw them off."

STRETCHING MINDS AND BODIES

As the repertoire diversified, so did the dancers, stretching the seams of their ballet technique into the off-center, non-vertical, asymmetrical, pelvis- and spine-oriented realms of modern and jazz. Dancer Stefani Schrimpf described learning Anna Sokolow's *Kaddish*: "Everything in ballet is usually controlled and contained and straight up and down. Your body knows what to do, but this is different. You're off-balance. Your head is back, and you're running backwards."

Avoiding injury and training for longevity is crucial in the professional dance world – akin to professional football in terms of the toll exacted on the body over the years. A typical day comprises eight hours of technique class and rehearsals, not counting performances. When teaching

34

Kimberly Cowen in "Hexentanz"
from *Six Solos of Consequence II* (2006)

Jerome Robbins's *The Concert* (2004)

Paris Wilcox and Lisa Choules in
Merce Cunningham's *Duets* (2003)

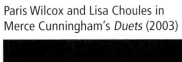

(top) Matthew Pawlicki-Sinclair in "Percussion IV"
from *Six Solos of Consequence II* (2006)

(above) Caitlin Cooney, Matthew Powell,
and Amber Metiva in Fernand Nault's
La Fille Mal Gardée (2006)

Whitener's *Haven* (2005)

company class, Whitener considers "how to prepare the body for a day's work. It's not just about warming up, but about organizing the body." He knows the frustration of injury, and credits teachers Robert Joffrey and Maggie Black as healthful influences. "If the repertory is varied, then the body learns," he continues. "Everybody who did the José Limón work [*The Moor's Pavane*] understands that they have more plié than they ever thought they did."

As the art and pedagogy of dance continue to evolve, practitioners employ smarter body mechanics and exhibit better technique and greater longevity. Kimberly Cowen and Christopher Barksdale, respectively sixteen- and nineteen-year veterans from the Bolender period, continue to delight audiences. Lisa Thorn, also a Bolender protégé, performed with the company for seventeen years, shifting to associate ballet mistress in 2004. Thorn and Ballet Master James Jordan share with Whitener the duties of teaching company class.

The dancers are learning all the time, but the tools are changing – from the body to dance notation to video. When in 2005 the company mounted Twyla Tharp's complicated *As Time Goes By*, the dancers learned it from watching Whitener and video documentation of the ballet.

NEW YORK REDUX

Before 2006, Kansas City Ballet had performed in New York on three occasions. Having debuted at the Brooklyn Center for the Performing Arts in 1987, it returned in 2004 to present Balanchine's "lost" *Renard* (reconstructed by Bolender) at Symphony Space. A year later KCB brought Twyla Tharp's *Nine Sinatra Songs* to the "Evening Stars" dance series at Battery Park – alongside such celebrated companies as Merce Cunningham, Lar Lubovitch, Momix, and David

Parsons. The coup: Not only was Kansas City Ballet asked to return, but it was invited to present an entire evening of work. "This constitutes our full-evening Manhattan debut," said Whitener in the *Star*, "and of course, we're thrilled."

In September 2006, the company opened the "Evening Stars" festival sponsored by New York's Joyce Theater, and the reception from critics and the crowd of two thousand was close to unanimous. Said Deborah Jowitt of the *Village Voice*: "When the Kansas City Ballet ends its evening with 'The Golden Section' from Twyla Tharp's *The Catherine Wheel*, the hordes camped out on the lawn might well believe that the heavens are displaying a particularly dazzling Perseid shower....The KCB dancers are splendid, and 'The Golden Section' turns them into conquerors." From *Pointe*: "Kansas City lit up the outdoor bandshell in Manhattan's Battery Park." From *danceviewtimes.com*, William Whitener's *Jaywalk* "caught fire in its witty, vibrantly rhythmic sections. It showcased Whitener's gift for manipulating a large ensemble through deft and interesting patterns, and made a bracing impact with its blend of contemporary technical pizzazz and nostalgic allusions."

Lisa Thorn and Russell Baker in Ruth Page's *Frankie and Johnny* (2001)

Stefani Schrimpf, Lateef Williams, and Catherine Russell in José Limón *The Moor's Pavane* (2007)

Kimberly Cowen in Jules Perrot and Jean Coralli's *Giselle* (2003)

36

Jeffrey Bentley, William Whitener (speaking), Tony Feiock, and Randy Clark at Whitener's tenth-anniversary performance (2006)

That appearance proved an eloquent preface for the next performance coup: The prestigious Joyce Theater invited Kansas City Ballet for a weeklong run as part of its regular season in March 2008.

FEATHERS IN CAPS

Sometimes national attention seems easier to attract than local, but in 2006, Kansas City Mayor Kay Barnes proclaimed "William Whitener Day," honoring the artistic director's ten-year anniversary with the company. Regionally Kansas City Ballet was among five winners of the 2002 Missouri Arts Award given by the Missouri Arts Council to institutions and individuals who have made "profound and lasting contributions to the cultural and artistic landscape of the state."

In 2006, six-year KCB veteran Matthew Powell was awarded a $10,000 Fellowship from the New York Choreographic Institute (an arm of New York City Ballet). While "In the Wings" gave Powell his first choreographic opportunity, the fellowship enabled him to create a piece on full company.

Another coup: the Kennedy Center for the Performing Arts invited Kansas City Ballet to perform *The Still Point* in its weeklong "Ballet Across America" program in June 2008, flanked by such companies as the Boston Ballet, Pacific Northwest Ballet, the Houston Ballet, and the Washington Ballet.

Perhaps KCB's biggest feather is measured by the numbers trying to get into the company versus the numbers leaving. The turnover has been minuscule – on average, two. As the company's reputation has spread nationwide, the numbers auditioning have doubled in the last two years. Between auditions in Kansas City, New York, and Chicago, visits to training programs at Pacific Northwest Ballet, North Carolina School of the Arts, and Ballet Austin, and video submissions, there are some 406 people vying for two spots.

BREATHING AND CHOREOGRAPHING

In Bill Whitener's new temporary office, cartons are stacked three high on the floor. "I love research," he says. "I have a big plastic tub that's filled to the brim with *Carmen* – the score, the text, all the notes I've taken." He has been turning *Carmen* around in his head for about ten years, haunted by the transcendent music of Georges Bizet in an arrangement by Rodion Shchedrin.

As rehearsal starts, dancers are draped on the barre, chatting and stretching. The atmosphere is professional, but not intimidating. Whitener works in street clothes and shoes, sometimes standing on a chair to get the overview. At the moment, the dancers are challenged by a sequence of leg, arm, and head changes, a Rubik's Cube of limbs. "New Version Number Eight!" he yells. People laugh. In Carmen's death scene, he asks leading lady Kimberly Cowen, "Are you comfortable?" after she has just been stabbed by partner Logan Pachciarz.

Whitener paraphrases mentor Tharp: A good cook uses everything. The skating he did as a kid informs a lift in the fight scene. Childhood string games (Cat's Cradle) become a metaphor as yards of red elastic around Carmen's waist is unwound by two suitors, entangling all three before becoming a tightrope. "At this point, choreographing really is like breathing," he says, then flips the simile back on himself: "Of course, sometimes you have trouble breathing."

Whitener's *Jaywalk* (2006)

Logan Pachciarz,
Kimberly Cowen,
and Luke Luzicka
in *Carmen* (2007)

Carmen went on to break all box-office records for any repertory show in Kansas City Ballet's forty-nine-year history. The ambitious hourlong piece was met with a standing ovation and hailed by the *Star* as "a visual feast with intricate choreography danced by three strong leads."

KANSAS CITY BALLET SCHOOL

After company rehearsal, the Kansas City Ballet School (KCBS) takes over as students in color-coded leotards stream into the studios (a room of green, a room of blue, a room of burgundy, a room of black). Suddenly the hallway is strewn with backpacks, and a cacophony of piano music bounces around in a kind of surrealistic dream.

Now six hundred students strong, KCBS boasts a staff of sixteen regular and ten guest faculty on two campuses. Following Director Karen Brown's tenure, Tenley Taylor has headed the school since 2004. Two tracks of study are offered: one for the aspiring professional, and the other for everyone else who wants to dance. Classes are offered in ballet, jazz, flamenco, modern dance, body conditioning, and yoga. Students audition to perform in the annual *Nutcracker* and occasionally augment the casts of other productions, such

as *Coppelia* and *The Sleeping Beauty*. The resident Midwest Youth Ballet, directed by veteran KCB dancer Alecia Good, offers other performance opportunities.

Begun in 1981 by Todd Bolender, the school still relies on the syllabus developed in that era to train dancers. "The legacy is in good hands," asserts Taylor, whose goal is to instill a love of dance in students. "They become the future custodians of the art form."

HOME AT LAST

When William Whitener first arrived, he was asked what, in a perfect world, he most wanted for the company. "A larger facility," he said, "with studios where dancers can never run out of space – fresh air and endless space."

After shuffling between eight makeshift locations over fifty years – from a garage to a fire station to its current warehouse – the Kansas City Ballet and school will at last have that space: sixty thousand square feet of it. The historic Union Station Power House will become the Ballet's permanent new home after a $20 million renovation. Opening in 2009 as the Todd Bolender Center for Dance and Creativity, the building will nearly double KCB's current number

FRED BLOCHER/
THE KANSAS CITY STAR

Whitener demonstrates a move for the bullfight scene with Matthew Powell in a *Carmen* rehearsal (2007)

of studios to seven, including a 180-seat informal theater for showings. With special soundproofing and joint-friendly sprung floors, the Bolender Center will boast skylights and long views. "It's the type of home that artists should have – a place that honors their work, values their sacrifice, and supports their creativity," says Executive Director Jeffrey Bentley.

As if that weren't enough, in 2010 the Kansas City Ballet will move its performances to the brand new, world-class Kauffman Center for the Performing Arts, designed by architect Moshe Safdie. The Ballet, along with the Kansas City Symphony and the Lyric Opera of Kansas City, will become the center's resident companies. Heading the $326 million project since her mother's death in 1995, Julia Irene Kauffman envisions the center becoming "a well-worn friend for Kansas Citians for many generations to come." Former Mayor Kay Barnes calls it the "linchpin" in the rebirth of downtown Kansas City.

The artistic triumphs of the Whitener era are reflected in a surge of organizational growth spurred in no small part by Jeff Bentley. In a twist of fate, Whitener encouraged the KCB board in 1998 to hire Bentley, the man who had recommended him to Winnipeg and with whom he had worked so well. Longtime General Manager Martin Cohen had decided after a decade with KCB to accept another offer, and the board sought a senior executive to complement Whitener's artistic strengths. Thus began a partnership that has steered Kansas City Ballet to its current high level of visibility and acclaim.

Now in the final phase of a $27 million capital and endowment campaign for its new home, KCB has in the last ten years eliminated all debt, more than doubled its operating budget to $5.5 million, and established an endowment of $4.5 million to ensure stability. "These days when a ballet company can have a fiftieth anniversary and still be financially healthy, it's really something to pay attention to," says Bentley. "While it doesn't follow that money will make great art, it's very difficult to put great art on the stage without money."

Throughout its history, the volunteer arm of the organization, Kansas City Ballet Guild, has raised a total of $4.3 million through Ballet Boutique sales and the Ballet Ball, which just marked its fortieth year. Now young professionals are getting involved through the BARRE, a social networking group (motto: "Art you can party with"). Three hundred hardy volunteers donate more than two thousand hours of service each year.

Bottom: Catherine Russell, Breanne Starke, Kimberly Cowen, Stefani Schrimpf, Geoffrey Kropp
Second row: Aisling Hill-Connor, Deanne Hodges, Caitlin Cooney, Juan Pablo Trujillo
Third row: Amber Metiva, Stayce Camparo, Christopher Barksdale
Fourth row: Matthew Pawlicki-Sinclair, Matthew Donnell, Matthew Powell, Angeline Sansone, Nick Kepley
Fifth row: Paris Wilcox and Chelsea Teel, Logan Pachciarz, Rachel Coats, Lisa Choules, Lateef Williams
Top: Luke Luzicka

THE GEOMETRY OF FLIGHT

Fifty years, three longtime artistic leaders. Those numbers alone communicate the ongoing endeavor called the Kansas City Ballet and the loyalty and longevity it inspires. Artistic directors have devoted their lives to shape its course. Executive directors and general managers have been known to stick around for a decade or two. Dancers have grown up in the company, moving from the stage to the studio, the costume shop, and the community. The first Clara in *Nutcracker* from Dokoudovska's era thirty years later becomes marketing director. Others fan out into the world, establishing schools and careers, enriching wherever they land.

After a half century, the Kansas City Ballet harbors 186 ballets from the far-flung ranks of Marius Petipa, August Bournonville, Isadora Duncan, George Balanchine, Merce Cunningham, Twyla Tharp, Anna Sokolow, Alvin Ailey, Lew Christensen, Bruce Marks, Jerome Robbins, Antony Tudor, José Limón, Bob Fosse, Agnes de Mille, Kathryn Posin, David Parsons, Mary Wigman, Loyce Houlton, and Daniel Nagrin.

Always, there is the work, uncountable and unseen: the everyday heroism of artists who bend and bleed for what they love, the devotion of the board and staff who grow the Ballet behind the scenes, the energy of volunteers who pull off the impossible, the generosity of supporters who remain on the donor columns, and the abiding mystery of the audience, who out there in the dark glimpse something transcendent. To all, a moment of silence. Then applause. ∎

Kimberly Cowen and Paris Wilcox
in Vincente Nebrada's
Lento...appassionato (2004)

Russell Baker's *Cloud Chamber* (2002)

Marius Petipa's *Paquita* (2004)

Courtney Bourman and
Sean Duus in Antony Tudor's
Offenbach in the Underworld
(1998)

Whitener's *Holberg Suite* (1998)

Christopher Barksdale, Amber Metiva,
and Logan Pachciarz in Twyla Tharp's
Deuce Coupe (2006)

41

Lila York's
Postcards from Home
(2004)

Kathryn Posin's
Stepping Stones
(2004)

Paris Wilcox and Aisling Hill-Connor in
Jerome Robbins's *Afternoon of a Faun* (2005)

Twyla Tharp's *The Catherine Wheel Suite* (2006)

William Whitener in rehearsal
with Kimberly Cowen and
Logan Pachciarz

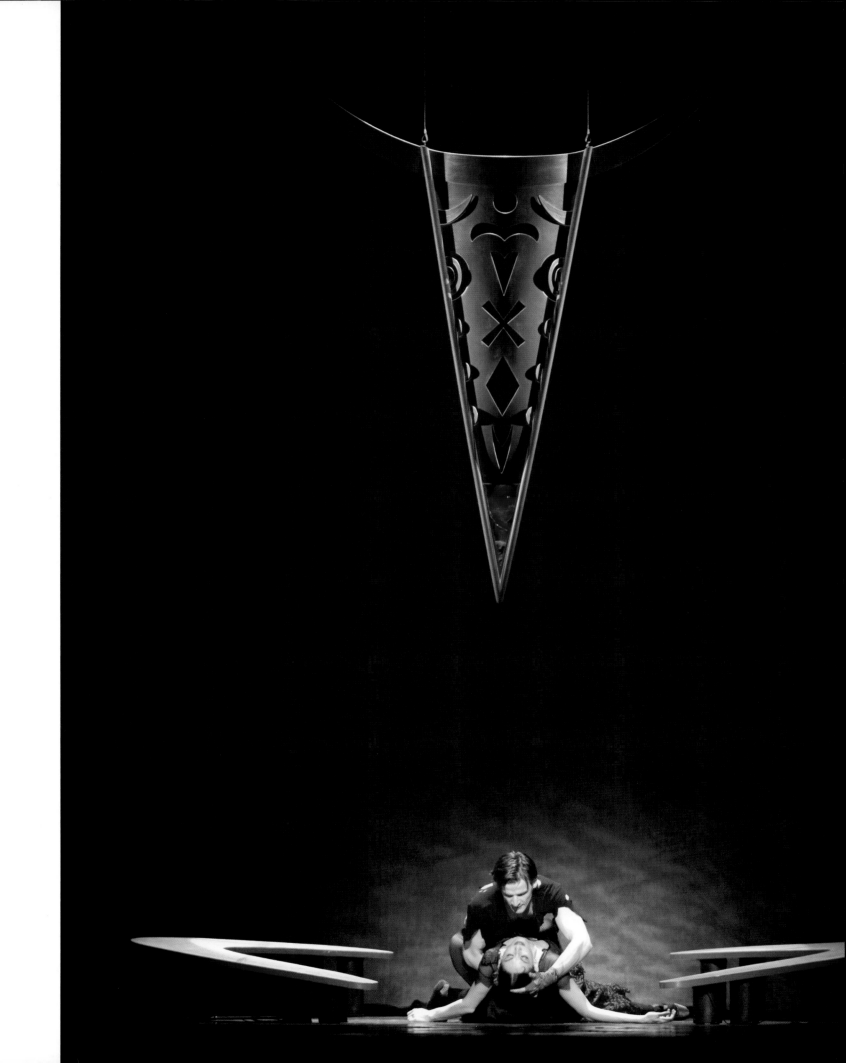

Logan Pachiarz and
Kimberly Cowen
in *Carmen* (2007)
Sets by Jason Pollen.

KANSAS CITY BALLET ROSTER
1957-2007

Our primary asset is priceless: talent. Nearly 550 people have danced with the Kansas City Ballet in its fifty-year history, bringing us glimpses of the sublime and a deeper experience of what it means to be embodied. We proudly acknowledge all the dancers who have graced the stage in our first half-century, and we have listed every name that our research could reveal, our contacts recall, and our early records rescue from obscurity. Any inadvertent omissions will be corrected in future printings.

Dante Adele	Blake Beardsley	David Braciak	Charlotte Cates	Kate Crews
Manuela Advincula	Julie Beck	Lise Brenner	Paul Chambers	Donald Crigger
Carter Alexander	Dawn Benson	William Brenner	Mary Eileen Chop	Lisa Cromwell
Dolly Allard	Sandahl Bergman	Gayle Brickman	Lisa Choules	Mervin Crook
Steven Allee	Fernando Bermudez	Anita Brock	Kathryn Christiansen	Nicholas Crumm
Dorman Allison	Kathleen Berry	Jana Brofman	Josh Christopher	William J. Crummett
Elaine Andalikiewicz	Annette Bertrand	Brook Broughton	Christian Claessens	Bryan Cunningham
Andrea Anderson	Christina Betts	Kelby Brown	Cheryl Clark	Gregory Cupp
Jody Anderson	Toinette Biggins	Patricia Brown	Christine Clark	Tim Cushing
Janet Andrade	Johnie Bishop	Todd Brown	Harvey Clark	Tom Cutler
Charlotte Andrews	Jennifer Black	Richard Bruce	Willie Clark	Joel Brent Czarlinsky
Nevin Arikoglu	Linda Black	Kelli Buckles	Rachel Coats	Donna Daly
Wendy Armacost	Susanne Black	Deena Budd	Cathy Coffman	Anita Davis
Karole Armitage	Daniel Blake	Igor Burlak	Judy Cole	Marty Davis
Gina Artese	Ray Blakey	Marilyn Butler	Nancy Cole	Susan Day
Joy Ashley	Nathan Bland	Linda Calvert	Jeremy Conner	Anne Dearman
Ricky Atwell	Beth Blattenberg	Diana Camacho	Sue Convin	Mary Kay Deboer
Edward Augustyn	Linda Bleish	James Cameron	Steven Cook	Kathi DeLapp
Jane Bair	Margaret Bohrer	Stayce Camparo	Caitlin Cooney	John Desiderio
Russell Baker	Elaine Bolend	Klas Campbell	Patrick Corbin	Grant Dettling
Sandie Balot	Visnja Boljkovac	William Campbell	Mindy Cooper	Michel DeVeers
Phillip Baltazar	Julia Bond	Nettie Capasso	Joan Cornall	Peggy Dewey
Brenda Barker	Reed Bondi	Julie Caprio	Sue Corwin	Robert Dio
Julia Barker	Frank Borg	William Carlyle	Lanny Costello	Bernadette Dona
Scott Alan Barker	Vicki Bouckhout	Benecia Carmack	Charlotte Cotes	Matthew Donnell
Christopher Barksdale	Courtney Bourman	Jean Carnall	Melody Courson	Kathy Doody
Donna Barton	Eric Bourman	Andrew Carr	Kimberly Cowen	Cynthia Draeger
Barbara Bayne	Benjamin Bowman	Dale Carter	Collin Cowley	Kim Driescher
Alejandro Bayo	Michelle Boyd	Randal Case	Joyce Crawford	Robert Drinan
Kim Bean	Matthew Boyes	Daniel Catanach	Annette Crespo	Richard Dryden

45

Logan Pachciarz
and Rachel Coats

Sandra Dugan	Judy Gillespie	Richard Hoiser	Karen Kreuter	Margaret May
William Dunne	Judy Glass	Shelly Holmes	Suzanne Kritzberg	Patricia May
Sean Duus	Stephanie Godino	Gerard Holt	Geoffrey Kropp	Jack Mayes
Teguin Dyer	Gene Goin	Duke Howz	Anthony Krutzkamp	Sharon McBee
Stephen Eads	Alecia Good	Da Dong Hu	Michael Kruzich	Jeffery McClure
Cathy Eberhart	Linda Gourley	Jeffrey Humfeld	Micah Kurtzberg	John McFall
Lanie Ebert	Trudie Green	Jack Hurley	Annette Laaser	Brian McGinness
Larc Edwards	Stephanie Greenwald	Dwight Hutton	William Laaser	Nathan McGinnis
Susan Eiler	Diana Gregory	Richard Isaac	Kathy Labovsky	Maura McKenna
Jeanne Elser	Marsha Grim	Nadia Iozzo	Kate Lacy	Dana McMahon
Monica Emilio	Elizabeth Grissinger	Byron Jacobs	Jorge Laico	Mike McMillen
Gloria English	Julie Gross	Kathy Jennings	Andrew Lamar	Gavin McNally
Marian Enochs	Angela Grove	Dana Jones	Sharon Lampros	Claire McNeiland
Carla Enos	Patricia Gruendahl	Pamela Jones	Judy Lants	Jan McQuerry
Hal Epstein	Lesley Haines	James Jordan	Diana Larsen	Janice Merlo
Ellen Erdman	Flora Ann Hall	Raymond Julian	Eve Lawson	Christi Merrill
Linda Eschenbaum	Sarah Hall	Renate Edwards Julian	Lanny Lea	Lisa Merrill
Jack Evans	Teresa Hall	Cynthia Kai	Zenia Lee	Robin Merrill
Cindi Ewing	Terry Hamilton	Andrew Kallem	Joyce Lemon	Agnes Meth
Kim Fahrlander	Trudy Hamilton	Peter Katris	Susan Lewis	Amber Metiva
Carol Williams Feiock	Michele Hamlett	Amber Kegley	Arthur Lindon Maddox	Natalie Milliard
Debbie Ferguson	Scott Hamlett	Paul Keller	Rodney Lloyd	Robert Mills
J. Fetterling	Lloyd G. Hammel	Melissa Kelly	Mike Loftus	Sheri Mitchell
Catherine Findlay	Martha Hancock	Allen Kemper	John Long	Tatsuo Mochizuki
Pamela Fink	Lesley Hanes	Nina Kennedy	Karen Lorhan	Vicki Molleson
Goddard Finley	Maryhelen Hanson	Roger Kent	Don Love	Cindy Monaco
Antoinette Finnell	Peggy Hanson	Nick Kepley	Steven Lumadue	Jean Montgomery
Mark Fischer	Elizabeth Hard	Greta Kerns	Luke Luzicka	Maura Montgomery
Jill Fleetwood	Susan Hard	Christine Kille	Karen Lynch	Barbara Morris
Elsa Fletcher	Lynda Harrell	Carol Kindell	Jennifer Lynn	Roland Morrisette
Pamela Ford	Hope Harris	Donna King	Linda Lyon	Susan Mortan
Ann Fouts	Muriel Harris	Kristin Kingsley	Wendy Macafee	Julie Morton
Arveila Frazier	Carol Harrison	Paul Kinola	Laurinda Mackay	Kay Moseley
Amy Freed	April Harry	Ned Kinter	Dana MacMahon	Pamela Moses
George Freelove	Cathy Hazeltine	Cliff Kirwan	Catherine Ann Mages	Milton Myers
Rick Friesen	Bryon Heinrich	Beverly Kitson	Ellen Makarewicz	Louise Nadeau
Patricia Frizzell	Patricia Herold	Betty Klein	Susan Manchak	Shahab Nahvi
Pattie Garland	Eileen Hertzel	Tamara Klein	Edward Mann	Eva Sue Newcomer
Homer Garza	Jean Hess	Gretchen Klockë	Kelly Mann	Jean Quick Niedt
Michael Gates	Harvey Hettick	Kendall Klym	Jerre Marcum	Heidi Noble
Diane Gaumond	Suzanne Hettick	Linda Knopke	Livia Marquez	Richard Noble-Orton
Emily Gaynor	Aisling Hill-Connor	Michael Koetting	David Martin	Mary Nowlin
Corinne Giddings	Judy Hilsabeck	Kathryn Eva Korslund	Renata Martinez	Jeanette Nuzum
Marsha Gifford	John Hirsch	Jennifer Kost	Gene Masoner	Sharon O'Dell
Paul Gilbert	Helen Hobe	Oliver Kovach	Kay Massman	Laura Oliver
Marilyn Gilkeson	Deanna Hodges	Brenda Krebs	Ernest Mavis	Jerry Opdenaker

Janet Oppenheimer
Jennifer Owen
Mitzie Pace
Logan Pachciarz
Dawn Parrish
Jodie Pattee
Matthew Pawlicki-Sinclair
Sally Pearson
Peter Pederson
Ron Pennington
John Pettingill
Molly Phillips
Liliane Pintar
Laura Ply
Peggy Ply
Dick Pond
Carolyn Potter
Matthew Powell
Wendy Powell
Carol Powick
Amy Pratt
Jeannine Price
Nathaniel Putnam
Sherrie Quinton
Robert Radford
Nancie Raether
Jamie Ralston-Wilson
Guillermo Ramirez
Phillip Rankin
Marilyn Rapier
Curt Ray
Mary Rayburn
Vicki Allen Reid
Dean Reiter
Vickie Rhoades
Edgar Richards
Paula Riegelman
Robert Rinehart
Margaret Roark
Anita Porte Robb
Jamie Roberts
Bea Robinett
Cecilia Rodarte
Heidi Rood
Helen Rosenthal
Carol Ross

Susan Ross
Robert Roth
Charles Roussin
Nancyelaine Rusk
Catherine Russell
Rebekah Sakati
Thomas Salken
Connie Salley
Jean Sandquist
Angelina Sansone
Arlene Saper
Shana Saper
David Scamardo
David Scanlon
Lois Scanlon
Sally Scanlon
Nancy Schmitz
Stefani Schrimpf
Wendy Scoops
Pamela Scott
Dean Serio
Roger Seward
Judy Shaper
Fairlea Sheehy
Yi Ming Shen
Kristin Shoaf-Roberts
Kim Shope
Debrah Felice Shore
Karen Shore
Steve Short
Frank Shott
Kathleen Shriner
Deann Silverman
Diana Silverman
Robert Skafte
Bonnie Skelly
Bradon Skolnik
Denise Small
Adrian Smith
Angela Smith
Dalton Smith
Don Smith
Erik Smith
Helene Smith
John Charles Smith
Steve Smith

Victoria Smith
David Smugar
Susan Soard
Mary Lynn Soli
Brian Staihr
William Stannard
Edwin Stark
Breanne Starke
Tom Steinhoff
Douglass Stewart
Jim Stoker
Lee Stone
Laura Stone
Melissa Stoneburn
Wendy Stoops
Susan Strain
Richard Sullivan
Robert Sullivan
Cindy Suske
Melinda Suske
Lisa Swanson
Curtis Sykes
Mike Tankersley
Judy Tarnawski
Tom Taylor
William Taylor
Chelsea Teel
Kateri Terns
Sydney Thomas
Lisa Thorn
Jack Townzen
George E. Tracy
Juan Pablo Trujillo
Edward Tuell
Anthony Tumbarello
Gail Turner
Deborah Ummel
Teresa Uribe
Lindy Van Ospel
Barbara Vaught
Francis Veyette
Larry Vincent
Howard Vogel
Russ Vogler
Ginger Vollrath
Robin Walker

Julie Wall
Francis Wardle
Stan Warmbrodt
Melissa Warner
Janet Watson
Nita Chyree Watson
Shirley Weaver
Carolyn Webster
Della Weinheimer
Carl Welander
John Wells
Karen Whitfield
Marvin Whitley
Keelan Whitmore
Paris Wilcox
Lateef Williams
Mary Jeanne Williams
Steve Wilson
William Woehrle
Sandra Wolf
Dana Wolfe
Mary Sue Woodcox
Regina Wray
Bruce Wright
Lauren Wright
Mark Wuest
Gail Yates
Trina Yatsko
Janet Young
Wanda Zackert
Holly Zimmerman
Jody Zirul

Josh Christopher

KANSAS CITY BALLET
REPERTORY LIST

TITLE	CHOREOGRAPHER	COMPOSER
À la Françaix	George Balanchine	Jean Francaix
A Midsummer Night's Dream	William Whitener	Felix Mendelssohn
A Summer's Day	Todd Bolender	Aaron Copland
Abendsterne Walzer	Shirley Weaver	Joseph Lanner
Acadian Sketches	Irmgard Altvater	Randall Thompson
Accordo	Christopher d'Amboise	Sergei Rachmaninoff
Aftermath	Dennis Landsman	Alan Hovhaness
Afternoon of a Faun	Jerome Robbins	Claude Debussy
Agon	George Balanchine	Igor Stravinsky
Allegro Brillante	George Balanchine	Peter Tchaikovsky
An American in Paris	Todd Bolender	George Gershwin
Apollo	George Balanchine	Igor Stravinsky
Arena	Todd Bolender	James Mobberley
As Time Goes By	Twyla Tharp	Joseph Haydn
Aurora's Wedding	Marius Petipa	Peter Tchaikovsky
Balletto	John Clifford	Ottorino Respighi
Billy the Kid	Eugene Loring	Aaron Copland
Black Swan Pas de Deux	Tatiana Dokoudovska	Peter Tchaikovsky
Bournonville Divertissements	August Bournonville	Paúlli/Helsted/Gáde
Brahms Paganini	Twyla Tharp	Johannes Brahms
Break of Day	Irmgard Altvater	Ernest Bloch
Café	Tom Steinhoff	Crabaugh
Cakewalk	Ruthanna Boris	Gottschalk/Kay
Caprice	William Whitener	Dmitry Kabalevsky
Carmen	William Whitener	Rodion Shchedrin after Georges Bizet
Carmina Burana	Paula Weber	Carl Orff
Carnaval	Fokine/Petipa	Robert Schumann
Carnival of the Animals	Zachary Solov	Camille Saint-Saëns
The Catherine Wheel Suite	Twyla Tharp	David Byrne
Celebration	Zachary Solov	Delius/Debussy
Celebration	Todd Bolender	Gershwin/Kay
Change of Heart	William Whitener	Works Recorded by Peggy Lee
The Chariot	Marjorie Mussman	Aaron Copland
Chopin Piano Pieces	Todd Bolender	Frédéric Chopin
Cirque de Deux	Ruthanna Boris	Charles Gounod
Classical Symphony	Todd Bolender	Sergei Prokofiev
Cloud Chamber	Russell Baker	Lou Harrison
Cobras in the Moonlight	Margo Sappington	Astor Piazzolla
Company B	Paul Taylor	Works Recorded by The Andrews Sisters
Con Amore	Lew Christensen	Gioachino Rossini

TITLE	CHOREOGRAPHER	COMPOSER
The Concert	Jerome Robbins	Frédéric Chopin
Concerto	Ruth Shafton	Peter Tchaikovsky
Concerto Barocco	George Balanchine	J. S. Bach
Concerto in F	Todd Bolender	George Gershwin
Coppélia	Todd Bolender	Léo Delibes
Coppélia, Act III	Todd Bolender	Léo Delibes
Coppélia, Act III	Ivanov/Sergeyev	Léo Delibes
Creation of the World	Todd Bolender	Darius Milhaud
Danse Concertante	Todd Bolender	Igor Stravinsky
Dark Elegies	Antony Tudor	Gustav Mahler
Debut at the Opera	Agnes de Mille	Léo Delibes
Designs in Shades of Baroque	David Howard	Johann Fasch
Deuce Coupe	Twyla Tharp	The Beach Boys
Divertimento	George Balanchine	Alexei Haieff
Divertimento #15	George Balanchine	Wolfgang Mozart
Divertissement	Zachary Solov	Léo Delibes
Divertissement d'Adam	David Howard	Adolphe Adam
Don Quixote (Pas de Deux)	after Marius Petipa	Ludwig Minkus
Donizetti Pas de Deux	Todd Bolender	Gaetano Donizetti
Donizetti Variations	George Balanchine	Gaetano Donizetti
Duets	Merce Cunningham	John Cage
The Dying Swan	Michel Fokine	Camille Saint-Saëns
Each and Every	William Whitener	Francis Poulenc
Enough Said	Clark Tippet	George Perle
Entrez Dans La Danse	Tatiana Dokoudovska	Aaron Copland
Feast of Ashes	Alvin Ailey	Carlos Surinach
Festival of Life	Joseph Albano	Compilation
Filling Station	Lew Christensen	Virgil Thomson
Firebird	Balanchine/Bolender	Igor Stravinsky
Flowers	Alvin Ailey	Joplin/Faith/Floyd
The Four Temperaments	George Balanchine	Paul Hindemith
Frankie and Johnny	Ruth Page	Jerome Moross
Gala Performance	Antony Tudor	Sergei Prokofiev
Galatea (Pas de Deux)	Todd Bolender	Franz Von Suppé
Gigue from Mozartiana	George Balanchine	Peter Tchaikovsky
Gingham Shift	William Whitener	Bela Fleck/Edgar Meyer
The Girl from Ipanema	Tatiana Dokoudovska	Antonio Jobim
Giselle	Perrot/Coralli	Adolphe Adam
Gloria	Lila York	Francis Poulenc
Grand Tarantella	Todd Bolender	L.M. Gottschalk
Great Galloping Gottschalk	Lynne Taylor-Corbett	L.M. Gottschalk
Handel Trio	Alonzo King	George Handel
Haven	William Whitener	Toru Takemitsu
Hey-Hay, Going to Kansas City	Donald McKayle	Jazz Compilation
Holberg Suite	William Whitener	Edvard Grieg
House of the Rising Sun	James deBolt	Scott Joplin
Iridice	Carlos Carvajal	Maurice Ravel
It Starts with a Step	Lotte Goslar	George Handel

Holly Zimmerman

49

KANSAS CITY BALLET REPERTORY LIST

Keelan Whitmore and
Stefani Schrimpf in
Nacho Duato's
Jardi Tancat (2005)

TITLE	CHOREOGRAPHER	COMPOSER
Jardi Tancat	Nacho Duato	Maria del Mar Bonet
Jaywalk	William Whitener	Jazz Compilation
Jinx	Lew Christensen	Benjamin Britten
Kaddish	Anna Sokolow	Maurice Ravel
La Boutique Fantasque	Tatiana Dokoudovska	Gioacchino Rossini
La Fille mal Gardée	Fernand Nault	Johann Hertel
La Sonnambula	George Balanchine	Rieti/Bellini
La Sylphide (Pas de Deux)	Bournonville	Hermann Lovenskjold
Lambarena	Val Caniparoli	J.S. Bach/trad. African
Lark Ascending	Bruce Marks	Ralph Vaughn Williams
Laurencia (Pas d'Action)	Chabukiani	Alexander Krein
Le Baiser de la Fée (Folktale)	Todd Bolender	Igor Stravinsky
Le Combat	William Dollar	Raffaello de Banfield
Lento e tempo é appassionato	Vincente Nebrada	Alexander Scriabin
Les Sylphides	Michel Fokine	Chopin/Glazounov
Lilac Garden	Antony Tudor	Ernest Chausson
Link	Alan Hineline	Luigi Boccherini
Lost in the Modern	Claire Porter	Monologue
Magic Hat	Vladimir Dokoudovsky	Giacchino Rossini
The Many Faces of Love	Isadora Duncan	Frédéric Chopin
Meditation	Jacques d'Amboise	Jules Massenet
Memoria	Alvin Ailey	Keith Jarret
The Miraculous Mandarin	Todd Bolender	Béla Bartók
Mobile	Tomm Rudd	Arum Khachaturian
The Moor's Pavane	José Limón	Henry Purcell
Mother Goose Suite	Todd Bolender	Maurice Ravel
Mozartiana	George Balanchine	Peter Tchaikovsky
Mystic Journey	Ronald Sequoio	Gustav Mahler
Napoli (Act III)	Bournonville	Helsted/Páulli
Nine Sinatra Songs	Twyla Tharp	Works Recorded by Frank Sinatra
Nutcracker	Tatiana Dokoudovska	Peter Tchaikovsky
Nutcracker	Todd Bolender	Peter Tchaikovsky
Offenbach in the Underworld	Antony Tudor	Jacques Offenbach
On the Boulevard	Whitener & Freydont	Ballroom Compilation
The Outing	Vladimir Dokoudovsky	Jacques Offenbach/J.P. Sousa
Paquita	Marius Petipa	Ludwig Minkus
Pas de Dix	George Balanchine	Alexander Glazounov
Pas de Quatre	Anton Dolin	Cesare Pugni
Pastorale	Francisco Moncion	William Turner
Percussion IV	Bob Fosse	Edgar Varèse
Piano Concerto #2	Robert Hill	Rolf Liebermann
Postcards from Home	Lila York	Marius Milhaud
Prodigal Son	George Balanchine	Sergei Prokofiev
Raymonda Variations	George Balanchine	Alexander Glazounov
Reflections	Eric Hyrst	Compilation
Rehearsal on Stage	Tatiana Dokoudovska	Waltz Compilation
Renard	George Balanchine	Igor Stravinsky
Rhapsody	Zachary Solov	George Gershwin
The River	Alvin Ailey	Duke Ellington
Rodeo	Agnes de Mille	Aaron Copland

TITLE	CHOREOGRAPHER	COMPOSER
Romeo & Juliet (Pas de Deux)	Michael Smuin	Sergei Prokofiev
Romeo and Juliet	Ib Andersen	Sergei Prokofiev
Round-up	Richard Holden	Hershey Kay
Rubies	George Balanchine	Igor Stravinsky
Ruse d'Amour	Fokine/Dokoudovska	Anatoli Liadov
The Scarlatti Dances	William Whitener	Domenico Scarlatti
Scotch Symphony	George Balanchine	Felix Mendelssohn
Sentinel	David Berkey	Johannes Brahms
Serenade	George Balanchine	Peter Tchaikovsky
The Sisters	Patrick Crommett	Arnold Schönberg
Slaughter on Tenth Avenue	George Balanchine	Richard Rodgers
Sleeping Beauty (Act III)	Marius Petipa	Peter Tchaikovsky
Song of Praise	Irmgard Altvater	G.F. Handel
Song of the Nightingale	George Balanchine	Igor Stravinsky
Songs in the Open Air	William Whitener	Felix Mendelssohn
Souvenirs	Todd Bolender	Samuel Barber
Square Dance	George Balanchine	Vivaldi/Corelli
Stars and Stripes (Pas de Deux)	George Balanchine	J.P. Sousa
Stepping Stones	Kathryn Posin	Joan Tower
The Still Point	Todd Bolender	Claude Debussy
Strange Hero	Daniel Nagrin	Kenton/Rugolo
Stravinsky Violin Concerto	George Balanchine	Igor Stravinsky
Suite Kander	Ann Reinking	John Kander
Swan Lake (Act II)	Marius Petipa, Lev Ivanov	Peter Tchaikovsky
Swan Lake (Act II)	George Balanchine	Peter Tchaikovsky
Swan Lake (Act II)	Kirov vers. Lev Ivanov	Peter Tchaikovsky
Swedish Songs	Bengt Jörgen	Traditional
Symphonic Metamorphosis	George Skibine	Paul I. Hindemith
Symphony	Zachary Solov	Wolfgang Mozart
Tangents	Eric Hyrst	Hawley Jackson
Tarantella	Tatiana Dokoudovska	Giacchino Rossini
Tchaikovsky Pas de Deux	George Balanchine	Peter Tchaikovsky
Tchaikovsky Suite/Dances	Todd Bolender	Peter Tchaikovsky
Three Courtesies	David Parsons	J. S. Bach
Toccata e due canzoni	Paula Weber	Bronislaw Martinu
Totem Ancestor	Merce Cunningham	John Cage
Traversal Tapestry	Vicki Allen Reid	Franz Schubert
Tribute to Muriel	Todd Bolender	Ludwig van Beethoven
Valse-Fantaisie	George Balanchine	Mikhail Glinka
Voyager	Todd Bolender	Leonard Bernstein
Western Symphony	George Balanchine	Hershey Kay
Widow's Walk	Lila York	Kurt Weill
Wingborne	Loyce Houlton	Antonin Dvorák
Witch Dance (Hexentanz)	Mary Wigman	Ernest Provencher
The World I Knew	Zachary Solov	Jules Massenet
Yes, Virginia, Another Piano Ballet	Peter Anastos	Frédéric Chopin
ZuZu Lounge	Margo Sappington	J.G. Esquivel
Zygosis	Zachary Solov	Igor Stravinsky

Chelsea Teel

51

Marius Petipa's *The Sleeping Beauty*
featuring Lisa Choules (center) with
Stefani Schrimpf and Juan Pablo Trujillo